920 Faherty, Justin L.
FAHERTY Movers and
shakers : men who
have shaped Saint
Louis.

MOVERS AND SHAKERS

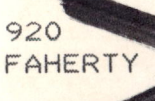

JEFFERSON COUNTY LIBRARY
NORTHWEST: HIGH RIDGE

This collection of thirty-eight biographies, each one a "Man of the Year," represents the best characteristics of St. Louis leadership. These men were selected by a committee of St. Louis businessmen, educators, and knowledgeable citizens. Honorees have demonstrated outstanding abilities in many fields and have contributed significantly to the quality of life in the metropolitan area.

The articles began in the *St. Louis Globe-Democrat* in 1955 and continued in the *St. Louis Post-Dispatch* after the *Globe's* demise.

The writers have been Justin L. Faherty (1955), David R. Brown (1956-74) and Mary Kimbrough (1975 to the present). Faherty and Brown are deceased. Kimbrough was named Media Person of the Year by the St. Louis Press Club in February 1992. Long considered one of the finest feature writers in St. Louis, Kimbrough has written several books and has taught her craft to aspiring writers for many years.

All articles have been edited for space and were updated by Dr. Verna Green Smith and Guin Tuckett Stemmler. Both editors are members of the sponsoring group, the Press Club of Metropolitan St. Louis, and and serve on its board as well as on the board of its charitable fund. Both are also members of the Missouri Press Women and the National Federation of Press Women. Smith, a volunteer in publications development for OASIS (Older Adult Service and Information System) is also active in Women in Communication. Stemmler served as a vice-president of Christian Board of Publication in St. Louis.

MOVERS AND SHAKERS

Men Who Have Shaped Saint Louis

Justin L. Faherty

David R. Brown

Mary Kimbrough

The Patrice Press
Tucson Arizona

Copyright © 1992
The Patrice Press

No part of this book may be reproduced, stored in a retrievable system, or transmitted in any form or by any means—electronic, mechanical, photocopying, recording, or otherwise—without the prior written consent of the publisher.

**Library of Congress
Cataloging-in-Publication Data**

Faherty, Justin L.
    Movers and shakers : men who have shaped Saint Louis / Justin L. Faherty, David R. Brown, Mary Kimbrough.
      p.   cm.
    ISBN 0-935284-96-6 : $14.95
    1. Saint Louis (Mo.)—Biography.   I. Brown, David R.
II. Kimbrough, Mary.   III. Title.
F474.S253F34   1992
977.8′66′0099—dc20   92-14252
                                                                                    CIP

The Patrice Press
1810 W. Grant Rd., Suite 108
Tucson AZ 85745
1-800-367-9242

Printed in the United States of America

Contents

1955	David R. Calhoun, Jr.	1
1956	Leif J. Sverdrup	5
1957	Ethan A. H. Shepley	12
1958	Stuart Symington	17
1959	Morton D. May	23
1960	Thomas B. Curtis	29
1961	August A. Busch, Jr.	35
1962	Edwin M. Clark	40
1963	Paul C. Reinert	46
1964	H. Sam Priest	52
1965	James P. Hickok	58
1966	Charles Allen Thomas	64
1967	Charles Powell Whitehead	71
1968	Frederic M. Peirce	75
1969	James S. and William A. McDonnell	81
1970	Maurice R. Chambers	90
1971	Howard F. Baer	96
1972	Harold E. Thayer	102
1973	W. L. Hadley Griffin	109
1974	Lawrence K. Roos	115
1975	Edwin S. Jones	121
1976	George H. Capps	127
1977	William H. Danforth	132
1978	Armand C. Stalnaker	138
1979	Edward J. Schnuck	144
1980	William H. Webster	150
1981	Zane E. Barnes	155
1982	Clarence C. Barksdale	161
1983	G. Duncan Bauman	167
1984	Sanford N. McDonnell	172
1985	Charles F. Knight	177
1986	Lee M. Liberman	182
1987	August A. Busch, III	188
1988	Robert Hyland	194
1989	Peter H. Raven	201
1990	Donald O. Schnuck	207
1991	William E. Cornelius	213

David R. Calhoun, Jr.

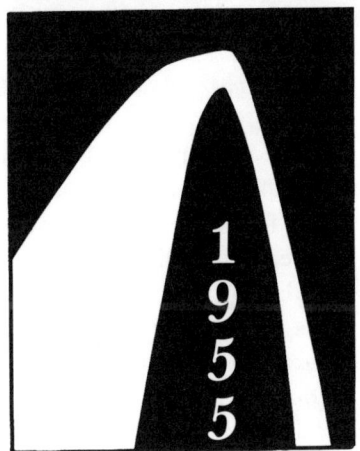

WHEN DAVID R. CALHOUN, JR., stepped forward at city hall to receive, along with Sidney J. Maestre, the St. Louis Award for 1955, it was the first time in his long and distinguished career as a St. Louis business and civic leader that he had been publicly rewarded for his continuous contributions to the growth and welfare of the metropolitan area.

A business executive once said: "In St. Louis all roads lead to Dave Calhoun."

As president of the St. Louis Union Trust Company and overseer of this city's largest estates, Calhoun was naturally interested in everything going on in the community. But his interest went well beyond the normal businessman's concern for such activities. He showed business shrewdness and organizational ability, which fit well into the civic enterprises he supported.

It is notable in Calhoun's case that the call for help was not just for his name—which is too true in so many civic endeavors. In every case, when the call went out for Calhoun, it was for work, not for a name on a committee.

The fact that he usually answered the call—and worked—reflected his deep interest in the city and his devotion to its progress.

Calhoun came by these prerogatives of business and organizational ability, plus his deep roots in St. Louis, directly from his father, who was one of the city's most distinguished merchants.

David R. Calhoun, Sr., came to St. Louis from New York in 1878 at the age of twenty to begin an association with a local dry goods firm—Ely, Janis & Co.—which was to last for forty-five years. In 1883 Calhoun, Sr., played a part in the reorganization of the firm, which then became incorporated as Ely & Walker Co.

Calhoun, Sr., was a dedicated businessman. His son, born on August 27, 1902, acquired this same zeal for business enterprise. Dave, Jr., was just a few months old when his father was elected president of Ely & Walker. The following year, the Calhouns moved to a magnificent estate on Clayton Road, later to become the Bogey Club.

As a youngster, Calhoun, Jr., attended the Academy of the Sacred Heart, then divided his high school days between two Eastern prep schools—Hill School at Pottstown, Pennsylvania, and Lawrenceville Academy at Lawrenceville, New Jersey. He spent one year at the University of Virginia, then gave up higher education for the business world. He joined his father at Ely & Walker in 1922. A year later he was elected a director of the firm.

Calhoun divided his time among many branches of the dry goods house during his eighteen years there. He was with the sales staff when his father died in 1925. Two years after his father's death, young Calhoun, then twenty-four, was appointed manager of the Walker Textile and Covering Company of Chicago, when Ely & Walker purchased this unit in 1925.

When the Chicago unit was closed in 1928, Calhoun returned to St. Louis and was placed in charge of the jobbing and ready-to-wear departments. He remained in that end of the business until 1935, when he was named vice-president and sales manager. Two years later, at its December meeting the directors of the St. Louis Union Trust Company, in addition to voting a Christmas bonus for employees and an extra dividend for stockholders, elected thirty-five-year-old David R. Calhoun, Jr., to their board.

The eyes of the business world were on this successful young merchant. Three years after Calhoun announced his resignation as Ely & Walker vice-president, he took up full-time association with the St. Louis Union Trust Company as vice-president.

Calhoun had hardly been indoctrinated into the trust business when war came. Less than a year after he was named vice-president of St. Louis Union Trust Company, Pearl Harbor changed the world.

Almost immediately the forty-one-year-old business executive was called on to take over and run the Trailer Company of America, a Cincinnati organization which had turned exclusively to making undercarriages for army and navy vehicles.

Calhoun was given a leave of absence from the trust company to carry on this war work, but he spent much time commuting between Cincinnati and St. Louis. In 1945, with war work at the trailer company just about at an end, he gave up the presidency there and returned to St.

Louis.

On January 17, 1946, David R. Calhoun, Jr., was elected president of the St. Louis Union Trust Company. There was some eyebrow raising within trust circles. Calhoun was just forty-three at the time. Not only was he young, but the wartime call on his services elsewhere had given him little opportunity for more experience.

As president of a trust institution devoted to the interests of St. Louis and the estates of St. Louis' most prominent citizens, and as a St. Louisan whose roots in civic and business enterprise went back more than three-quarters of a century, Calhoun gave far more than the usual amount of time to civic affairs during those years.

Actually, Calhoun was the man behind the scenes. When someone needed to be brought into the fold or brought into line, when there was a really big business deal to be consummated, when two opposing groups had to be brought together, when a long-range plan of action had to be mapped out, someone was usually asked to call on Dave Calhoun and see if he was available.

For instance, when the Saint Louis Symphony Orchestra needed new and vibrant blood to keep it in existence, Calhoun was called on to find the man for the job. He persuaded Edwin J. Spiegel, president of Gaylord Container Corporation, to take over the task.

In 1953, as the retirement of George C. Smith as president of the chamber of commerce became imminent, Calhoun began negotiations with the best man he could think of to fill the job and give the chamber new life and vitality. He went straight to Aloys P. Kaufmann, former St. Louis mayor, and lined him up for the presidency. Then he sold the idea to the chamber.

The back-stage creation of the United Fund was also turned over to Calhoun. So many of Calhoun's jobs came as a problem that needed a solution. He studied the issue and found an answer.

Calhoun was in on Civic Progress, Inc., from its beginning. He was one of the original eight asked by Mayor Joseph M. Darst to form the nucleus of a non-profit civic organization of business leaders designed to foster broad, long-range civic improvement. When Mayor Raymond R. Tucker came into office in 1953, he heartily endorsed the plan and Civic Progress, Inc., became a reality. There was some suggestion that membership in the organization should be all inclusive and a list of some 300 names was presented at one time. Calhoun could not see such an unwieldy number. It was his idea that membership in such an organization should be small enough to be workable, fewer than twenty members, for example. He was named chairman of the membership committee, and Civic Progress wound up with a compact, hard-hitting group of eighteen men.

Another important group which he headed was the mayor's traffic committee, which was under Calhoun's leadership in the mid-1940s. The report that his committee presented brought both commendation and condemnation. As Calhoun reminisced, "It takes courage to tackle the traffic problem. You are sure to please some and step on others' toes."

In addition to serving as president of the St. Louis Union Trust Company and serving his community, Calhoun was a director of numerous business corporations and served as a director of such widely varied civic organizations as the Chamber of Commerce, the Saint Louis Symphony Society, the Municipal Opera, the Crime Commission, the Zoological Society, the Central Institute for the Deaf, Boys Town of Missouri, the St. Louis Council of World Affairs, and the Urban Redevelopment Corporation. He was a vice-president of the Mid-American Jubilee, which was presented on the riverfront in 1956.

Lucy Whitelaw Terry, who became Mrs. Calhoun in April 1926, was a perfect complement to her husband. She was one of St. Louis' hardest working community volunteers and, like her husband, was more "behind the scenes" than "front and center."

How did a business executive find time for so many activities?

"First of all, he must have a good organization of his own," said Calhoun. "Then he must have a great interest in the projects he takes on."

Dave Calhoun had a tremendous interest in St. Louis—both as a businessman and as a citizen of the community. "A community the size of ours cannot stand still," he said. "It must plan and grow. That is everybody's job."

David R. Calhoun, Jr., died May 15, 1974.

Leif J. Sverdrup

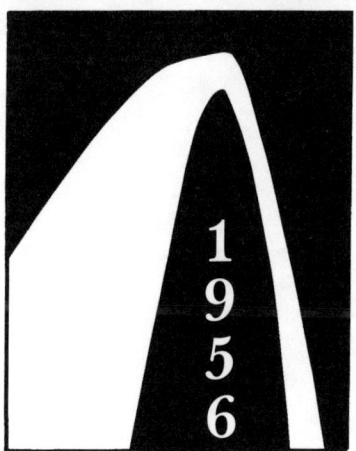

A HEARTY SON OF NORWAY, who came to this country as a visitor in his youth and stayed on to become one of the nation's great military heroes, one of the world's outstanding engineers, and one of this community's most dedicated business and civic leaders was Maj. Gen. Leif J. Sverdrup.

He determinedly and indefatigably put through, as chairman of the chamber of commerce traffic committee, the first solid steps toward dissolving the area's traffic bottlenecks. At the same time, he continued his amazing military record, established in World War II, by devoting countless hours to service as commanding general of the 102nd division, chairman of the advisory committee on National Guard and Reserve Affairs and work as a committee member of the Reserve Force Policy Board.

He culminated a twenty-eight-year career as a wizard of engineering with the assignment to build the unbelievable twenty-eight-mile roadway across the menacing Chesapeake Bay from Norfolk to Cape Charles, Virginia.

His busy days also included time for other community projects, including service with the Boy Scouts; the betterment of international relations through his work in exchange fellowships and in immigration problems; a happy home life; a vigorous program of outdoor recreation; and development of one of the state's most important cattle farms.

The trouble with Jack Sverdrup was that his beginning almost eluded us. To know the St. Louis Sverdrup well, it is necessary to know Norway's Sverdrups.

A great-great-grandfather—whose portrait hung over the fireplace of the Sverdrup home—wrote the constitution of Norway. That distin-

guished patriot also helped put the constitution into effect and was a leader in developing national improvements.

The next generation of Sverdrups turned from national affairs to religion. Grandfather Sverdrup—Dr. Harold U. Sverdrup—was a leading churchman who wrote the edition of Luther's Small Catechism, which was used widely in both Norway and the United States in the training of the young for confirmation in the Lutheran Church. He sired eight children, all of whom either became clergymen or, in the case of the daughters, married clergymen.

One of those eight—Dr. Edward Sverdrup—was stationed on the little island of Ytre Sulen, south of Bergen. There Leif Johan was born on January 11, 1898. Ten years later the family moved to Oslo, where Dr. Sverdrup began work with the Independent Theological School's *Menighets Fakultet.* Later, General Sverdrup's father became professor of church history and eventually president of the school, serving in that capacity until his death in 1923.

When he was fourteen, Leif Johan decided it was time to prove to his family that he was becoming a man and was capable of accepting the responsibilities of a man. He bade adieu to his parents and the tutor of his elementary student days and took himself off to the farmlands of Norway. A week later he had earned the munificent sum of ninety cents as a harvest hand. On Saturday evening he slicked down his hair, donned his best attire, and visited the nearest village. There he spent the entire ninety cents for a photograph of himself, which he then bore proudly back to Mama.

In 1914 young Sverdrup went to the United States—to Minnesota, where so many others of Viking blood had found new homes. He became a student at Augsburg College. From Augsburg he went on to the University of Minnesota, eventually earning both his B.A. and M.S. in engineering. With Europe at war, young Sverdrup found neither the opportunity nor a great desire to return to Norway. There was much to be done in this new country.

During the summers, there was the need to work in the harvest fields. Leif did that with a vengeance and a forcefulness that reflected his Viking blood. Then, when age permitted, there was the chance to serve this new country in military service. He enlisted in the U.S. Army—though still not a citizen—and eventually found himself located at Camp Devers, Massachusetts, and a candidate for officers' school.

Soon Leif Johan Sverdrup, a six-foot, blond son of Norway, received citizenship papers indicating that he was a five-foot-six, black-haired, swarthy newcomer who had just renounced allegiance to the sultan of

Turkey. Sverdrup took the papers to his commanding officer and complained.

"Don't worry," the officer put him off, "you're a citizen now."

"But," protested Sverdrup, "I want to be able to show them in the future—proudly. They're incorrect. How can I be proud of inaccurate papers?"

He continued his protest until his superior officer gave in. A general order went out and all those with incorrect papers were herded back to Boston. There was a reshuffling of documents and eventually everyone—including Leif Johan Sverdrup—wound up with accurate records of their new citizenship.

When World War I ended, Sverdrup returned to Minneapolis to finish his education at the University of Minnesota. During that period he met Helen Egilsrud—his Molly. Molly had been born in Tromso, Norway, the daughter of a physician who carried on his practice in the dim twilight beyond the arctic circle.

Dr. Egilsrud had come to Minnesota, and his daughter had fastened her chariot to his star. She was studying to become a doctor when she met that other Viking—the engineer from Oslo. They were married November 26, 1924.

The union brought together two diverse but delightfully compatible components of family life. One the one side there was the adventurous engineer. On the other side, Molly's father was a humanitarian doctor; her mother, Helen ("We couldn't have two Helens around the house, so I became Molly," explained Mrs. Sverdrup), had a deeply inbred artistic talent.

Jack Sverdrup worked for the Minnesota Highway Commission after he completed his studies. Then, in 1922 he read that the state of Missouri was creating a highway commission to build the roads that the state needed so badly.

"A new commission means a start from scratch," he reasoned. He applied for a job and became a designer in the bridge department. During the next year he worked on plans for highway bridges at Waverly, Lexington, Glasgow, and Boonville. Then, in 1924, he was appointed chief bridge engineer.

In the months that followed he gave serious consideration to a question which he frequently presented to himself: "Look, old boy, where do you really want to go?"

Sverdrup put the answers together and found that he wanted to own his own company. To do that, he determined three steps were necessary. First, he must have a little money to get started; that could be taken care of by frugal living and sound investment. Second, he must absorb all there was to know about the business. And third, he must meet people—attend every engineering meeting and convention he could.

Within three years, Sverdrup decided he had reached his first immediate goal. He returned to Minnesota to seek out a former professor, John Ira Parcel. Together they formed the firm of Sverdrup & Parcel, Inc., engineers and architects, with offices in St. Louis.

For the first ten years of its existence, the firm of Sverdrup & Parcel concentrated its efforts almost entirely on bridge building. The first structure these engineers completed was the bridge at Hermann, Missouri. The following year they spanned the Missouri River again, at Nebraska City, Nebraska. That same year, Sverdrup & Parcel built the unique upside-down Grand Glaize Bridge over an arm of the Lake of the Ozarks.

During the early depression days, the young firm received only one contract; but in 1933 there were five bridges to be built and Sverdrup & Parcel went into high gear.

On December 7, 1941, Leif Johan Sverdrup found himself in the Fiji Islands. Two months earlier, the U.S. Army Engineers had asked him to construct a string of air bases for a plane-ferrying route to the Philippines and Australia. He was in Fiji, involved in this task, when the Japanese struck Pearl Harbor.

Still a civilian, Sverdrup hopped to Australia to plan a vital supply highway from Melbourne to Darwin. He had hoped to return from the South Seas project for Christmas. That was not to be. Sverdrup got back from the South Pacific only for a brief visit during World War II. That was early in 1942, when he flew back to Washington to be commissioned a colonel in the U.S. Army Corps of Engineers. Colonel Sverdrup then went back to the South Pacific to see what he could do about helping to win the war.

Those were grim days. He was ordered to make a reconnaissance trip to explore the possibility of building a road across New Guinea, east of the Japanese positions, along which troops could be moved to attack the enemy's stronghold.

For six weeks, afoot and accompanied by one guide, he cut his way through the jungle, eluding the enemy, battling malaria and winning the confidence of the natives he met en route.

Once back from this grueling mission, Colonel Sverdrup reported that the road project was not feasible. Instead, he recommended to Gen. Hugh Casey, Douglas MacArthur's chief engineer, that a series of airstrips be hacked out of the jungle at points he had spotted on his trip.

General MacArthur studied the plan on a map, then turned to Colonel Sverdrup, poked a finger into the colonel's shoulder and said, "Approved. And you'll do it."

Back into the same jungles went Sverdrup, this time with a contingent of 297 natives. Thus the battle to hold New Guinea advanced under Sverdrup's ingenious engineering methods. The toehold became solid.

Sverdrup rose from colonel to brigadier general, then to major general. Seldom in American military history had a man who was not a professional soldier risen so quickly.

Soon General MacArthur was ready to return to the Philippines. General Sverdrup went with him and on January 21, 1945, at the direction of President Roosevelt, became the first American cited in the Luzon campaign. The order for his Distinguished Service Cross read:

> For extraordinary heroism in action against the enemy at Lingayen, Luzon, Philippine Islands, on January 9, 1945. Landing with the first wave of assault troops and with complete disregard for his own safety, he proceeded immediately to render invaluable assistance in the seizure of the vital Lingayen Air Field. General Sverdrup's exceptional courage, initiative and determination contributed immeasurably to the successful accomplishment of the mission.

General Sverdrup went all the way to victory with General MacArthur and was on hand for the signing of the peace treaty with the Japanese aboard the *U.S.S. Missouri*.

When the general returned to business after the war, the firm of Sverdrup & Parcel extended its field of operations from building bridges. One of the largest contracts he ever took on, together with others, was the assignment from the king of Saudi Arabia in 1947 to build, at a cost of more than $250 million, a 671-mile trans-Arabian oil pipeline, auxiliary railroads, piers, roads, hospitals, and housing developments to facilitate bringing the product of the world's richest oil field from central Arabia to the Mediterranean Sea.

In 1950 the U.S. Air Force gave Sverdrup & Parcel another giant assignment—the design, construction, and operation of the $200 million Arnold Engineering Development Center near Tullahoma, Tennessee. There, in the early days of the jet age, the wizard of jungle warfare was called on to produce wind tunnels and other testing and research equipment for supersonic planes, missiles, and propulsion systems that might be used in any future military necessity.

From Venezuela to Thailand to Saudi Arabia and on to Potosi, Missouri; from a small, rural parochial school to the new look at Busch Stadium; and on to the vast supersonic testing ground at Tullahoma, Sverdrup & Parcel solved major engineering problems. Yet Sverdrup remained a loyal St. Louisan.

He served the St. Louis area in countless ways, despite the heavy toll on his time, in Boy Scout work (for which he received the Silver Beaver Award, highest honor paid to adult leaders), in aviation, in engineering, and in civic planning.

He was the first chairman of the Bi-State Development Commission, set up by the states of Missouri and Illinois to do for greater St. Louis what the New York Port Authority did for that metropolitan area. Despite the fact that the commission was hamstrung by Missouri legislation which made it almost impossible to borrow money, the agency built and put into operation the harbor wharf at Granite City.

What sort of a person was this human dynamo, whose untiring drive did so much for the city, state, and nation? Where did he get the time and energy for all this activity?

"He was a wonderful family man," said Mrs. Sverdrup. "He had the happy faculty of leaving business and all his other projects at the office. He was a husband and father who was with his family in spirit all the time."

In 1950 the Sverdrups bought a farm near Washington, Missouri, and there General Sverdrup brought an international champion Black Angus heifer and became one the nation's leading breeders of this type of cattle.

In his office Sverdrup liked to direct the attention of visitors to a unique spot on the world globe. There, high above the arctic circle, far above the most remote Canadia outposts, a strong of dots was labeled, "Sverdrup Islands." They were discovered by a great-uncle of his, the noted Norwegian explorer, Otto Sverdrup.

"That's where I'm going to retire someday," mused the general. "Far from everything."

The next question was a natural: "When do you expect to retire, General?"

Leif Johan "Jack" Sverdrup had no direct answer. "Life is so fascinating," he said. "I just like to waltz around in unknown pastures."

Maj. Gen. Leif Johan Sverdrup died January 2, 1976.

Ethan A. H. Shepley

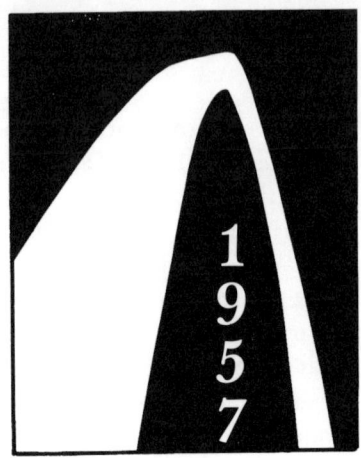

IT WAS 1930, A BLEAK YEAR. The stock market was in ruins and depression was creeping over the land. People were hungry and shelterless; a black winter was just ahead.

A young St. Louis lawyer who happened to be in Arizona received an urgent message to hurry home. Without his knowledge or consent, he had been made president of the Community Chest, which was about to conduct its annual campaign.

It was not the kind of job that attracted applicants. Times were hard, and money was scarce. The campaign could turn out to be a dismal flop. But Ethan A. H. Shepley promptly accepted the challenge, and at the age of thirty-four became the city's youngest Community Chest president.

He whipped the frazzled organization into shape, took charge of the campaign himself, and worked day and night pleading for funds. After much travail, the drive reached its goal of $2,250,000, but young Shepley had campaigned so tenaciously that he neglected his own business and saw the inside of his downtown law office only five times during the entire drive.

Already underway when that campaign ended was a varied and productive career that was to make a sizable impact on this community. Shepley built a distinguished career as a lawyer, yet whenever needed, he took time from his profession to give civic leadership to his community. At one time he spent a year helping frame a new state constitution, and his compensation barely covered his living expenses.

While working long and hard for civic progress, he also served his church well. He took a constructive interest in national, state, and community politics, and never ceased to urge the use of the vote by all citizens.

When well into middle age, Shepley left his prosperous law practice—at first reluctantly—to become chancellor of Washington University. He made this drastic change in his life because the faculty wanted him and because he saw a wider field for service.

As far back as anyone remembered, the ancestors of Ethan Shepley were learned in the law. His great-grandfather was chief justice of the Supreme Court of Maine, the state from which the paternal side of his family came. His grandfather was a well-known St. Louis attorney. His father was John Foster Shepley, a lawyer and chairman of the board of the St. Louis Union Trust Company. Young Ethan grew up to become an esteemed figure in the courtrooms of the city and state. He loved and respected the law that was so inseparably a part of his family history.

Shepley's mother, directly descended from history's Ethan Allen, was a daughter of Ethan Allen Hitchcock, a onetime ambassador to Russia and secretary of the interior in the William McKinley and Theodore Roosevelt cabinets.

Ethan was born May 3, 1896, and spent his early childhood in the family home in Vandeventer Place. Later the family moved to Portland Place. After elementary education in St. Louis, young Shepley attended Hill School, a preparatory academy at Pottstown, Pennsylvania, near Philadelphia.

His attendance there was to affect his life. At a house party arranged for the students, he met Sophie Baker, one of six sisters who lived in nearby Philadelphia. From prep school and the start of that romance, Shepley went to Yale, where he made the varsity baseball team. During his chancellorship, he could sometimes be spotted in the stands watching the Washington University nine play.

Shepley was at Yale, traveling with the baseball team when the United States entered World War I. He came home to St. Louis, volunteered, and was commissioned a second lieutenant. He did not get overseas, an eventuality he regretted at the time.

After the war, Shepley returned to Yale and completed his undergraduate work. Later he entered Harvard Law School. He stayed one year and then transferred to Washington University for the remaining two years of law school. He formally graduated in 1922, but a year before that, he passed the bar examination and joined the law firm of Nagel & Kirby, attending school in the mornings and working afternoons. By 1931 he had been admitted to partnership, and the prominent law firm of Nagel & Kirby became Nagel, Kirby & Shepley.

When World War II came along, the man who had missed a chance to become a hero in France in 1918, became a colonel of the First

Missouri Infantry Reserve and served in that capacity throughout the conflict, with the exception of the year spent as a delegate to the state constitutional convention. This home-guard service meant weekly drill at the St. Louis Armory.

The romance that started in prep school with Sophie Baker culminated in marriage in 1921. The oldest of their four children was Ethan A. H. Shepley, Jr., a lawyer and banker. Their daughter, Sally, who was a Veiled Prophet queen, became Mrs. William G. Moore, Jr. The other children were Louis Baker Shepley and Sophie Stevens Shepley.

In 1953 Shepley was a founder of Civic Progress, Inc., an organization of prominent citizens created to draft long-range plans for the city. An Episcopalian, he served as senior warden of Christ Church Cathedral, which his family attended for four generations. Politically, Shepley was a Republican.

When asked how he came to be involved in so many public problems at a loss of his own time and convenience, he had to search momentarily for an answer. "Well, I guess you do things in life that you like and that are interesting to you," he conjectured at length. "I was always interested in people and their problems."

Early in his law career Shepley became involved in the public welfare, and in the late 1920s found himself on the budget committee of the Community Chest. This committee had the tough chore of distributing the available funds among needy agencies. It was soon evident that such an able, useful, and willing young lawyer should be chairman of this crucial committee.

It became something of a habit from then on to call on him when someone was needed to devote time and talent to some public problem. And more often than not, he responded.

Through the years his time, energy, and sagacity were put to use for the public good in a variety of activities which ranged from helping pick the first St. Louis County police board to helping shape a new state constitution. He served on and headed important citizens' committees, two of them appointed by mayors, to ponder ways of rescuing the municipal government from recurrent economic plights.

One task presented to him changed his life. He was asked to give some of his time to help Washington University in a pinch. He did. And the upshot was that lawyer Shepley suddenly became Chancellor Shepley, administrative head of a major university.

Why did he quit his law practice of thirty-three years? Because he believed he could do more worthwhile things in education than in law.

His career change really began in 1940, when he was elected to the

Washington University Corporation. He wasn't elated about the election. At that time he had many other duties and felt he was being overloaded. For about a year he refused to attend any meetings of the corporation, but he softened eventually. By 1951 he had showed such interest that he was made president.

Fate was at work. The world renowned nuclear physicist, Dr. Arthur Holly Compton, was then chancellor and announced he would retire in 1953. A committee appointed to find a new chancellor set such high qualifications that fulfillment was almost impossible.

No successor had been found by the time Compton retired. In this emergency, the board did the usual thing. They called on Ethan Shepley for help. And, as usual, Shepley consented. He turned his law practice over to his partners and settled down to the job of acting chancellor, hoping the committee would soon find a permanent replacement.

But the screening committee could find no adequate successor to Compton. At the same time, an Ethan Shepley boom spread among the applicants. They liked his administrative ability. He lacked experience as an educator, but he was willing to learn.

Acting Chancellor Shepley had no interest in becoming the permanent chancellor. He wasn't a candidate; he didn't meet the requirements. Still, the faculty favored him overwhelmingly, and when the screening committee was convinced of that, the chancellorship went to Ethan Shepley. A change came over him. His reluctance disappeared.

"When I learned that the faculty actually wanted me, it became a very attractive job. I entered it with joy and found it the most challenging and satisfactory work I have ever done."

A university administrator must get money as well as spend it. Endowments, gifts, and bequests kept the school on the right side of the ledger. The university thrived under the Shepley administration.

Was the man who was steeped in generations of law tradition sorry he left the courtroom for the campus? No, he said emphatically.

"This is a useful job. What can be better than to make it possible for young people to benefit by the educational process, to make their lives happier and more worthwhile. The universities provide the leadership of the future.

"I want to go on doing this job for years, until retirement sends me on my way. And then? . . . Then I think I'll go back to practicing law."

Ethan A. H. Shepley died on June 2, 1975.

Stuart Symington

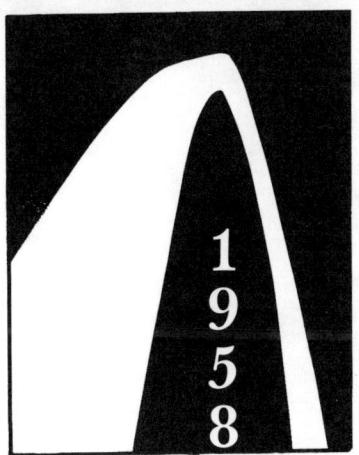

1958

At the end of the Great Depression, an engaging stranger showed up in St. Louis. He walked into a dreary industrial plant, hung up his hat, and took over a big job. The job was to make the ailing company well. It looked as if it would be a long job, so he brought his family from the East, bought a home, and settled down.

In business circles along the Eastern seaboard, this newcomer was favorably known and regarded as quite a remarkable fellow for his thirty-seven years. But in St. Louis he was a stranger, and his first requirement was to introduce himself to almost everyone.

His name, he said with a warming smile and handshake, was W. Stuart Symington, late of Maryland and New York. To those who met him for the first time, he was a provocative fellow—tall, lanky, good-looking—with a sort of urgency about him. He seemed like a man who could get things done, and fast. He *did* get things done.

In the years after Symington arrived in St. Louis, he distinguished himself nationally in each of three separate careers—industry, government, and politics. He reached such public esteem that in some quarters he was considered a good candidate for his nation's highest office.

Stuart Symington was long zealous for the strength and safety of America. More than anyone else in the postwar years, he was an unsleeping sentry, watching the nation's ramparts and crying out a warning that a poised predator would pounce the moment it achieved military superiority. As a high defense official and then as a member of the U.S. Senate, he preached with a prophet's fervor against complacency and unrealistic optimism.

Prodigiously informed on military matters, he prodded development of the weapons of the future—missiles, nuclear-powered planes, and outer

space satellites. When the Senate set up an unprecedented thirteen-man congressional group—the outer space committee—with broad powers to legislate on all matters dealing with space exploration, Senator Symington was named a member, even though he lacked seniority.

In the Senate he followed his sincere convictions even when they crossed party lines. President Dwight D. Eisenhower's bill to revamp and streamline the sprawling defense department along more efficient and economical lines found a stalwart champion in Symington, who bore the major part of the burden in carrying it through the Senate to an 80-to-0 victory.

One of Missouri's most distinguished senators in modern times, Symington served his state well in seeking to solve individual and collective problems. The year 1958 was one of the most successful and productive in congressional legislation benefiting the St. Louis area, and much credit for this went to the tireless efforts of Senator Symington.

The long-stagnant proposal for the Jefferson National Expansion Memorial on the riverfront began moving in Washington under the incessant hammering of the senator from Missouri. In the end, Congress authorized spending $17,230,000 on the memorial project, and dirt began moving for the first time.

A long fight brought another success—Congress approved spending the necessary federal funds to give St. Louis a badly needed new federal building and records center. Congress also voted funds for Missouri flood control, which enabled St. Louis to begin work on an extensive river program to protect the city from a fifty-two-foot flood stage. In Washington he helped in the fight for better airline service for St. Louis, which was long the victim of discrimination.

The new century, which would be full of technological and scientific miracles, was just getting underway when William Stuart Symington was born at Amherst, Massachusetts. This was an out-of-the-way place for him to be born—so far north—because he came from old families of Maryland and Virginia and had two grandfathers who had fought for the Confederacy.

Stuart was still at Yale when something happened that changed the direction of his life. While at home in Baltimore, he went to a debut party in nearby Washington. Expecting no more than a pleasant evening, he met a vibrant girl named Evelyn Wadsworth. She had a formidable list of things in her favor. She had a vivacious and fascinating mind. Her family was patrician and prominent. Her father was Senator James W. Wadsworth from New York, who later also served for many years as a congressman. Her grandfather, John Hay, had been a private secretary to Abraham Lincoln and, many years later, President William McKinley's secretary of state.

Symington had planned to study law and enter a partnership with his father. But love altered things. He trimmed his plans to be in geographical proximity to Evelyn, whose family home was in Geneseo, New York.

With Yale behind him in 1923, Symington decided to go to work for one of his well-to-do uncles, who owned the Symington Company in Rochester, New York, manufacturer of railroad equipment. In the best tradition, he started at the bottom.

On March 1, 1924, there was a dazzling wedding in Washington. Evelyn Wadsworth became Mrs. W. Stuart Symington and went home to a modest two-room apartment in Rochester. The young husband drove hard toward the future. After supper he studied, attending classes in mechanical and electrical engineering three nights a week. A fourth night he worked on a correspondence school metallurgy course.

His determination, his inherent qualities, and his ascetic preparation were soon to carry him to distinction and fortune in the field of industry. In the next half-dozen years, there was a blurred succession of companies which he headed or identified with, mostly owned by his uncles.

Along in the early 1930s the attractive and multi-talented Evie Symington got into the limelight. The Symingtons were living in New York at the time, and they had two sons. At a charity affair one night, Evie was asked to sing. She did, in a low-key husky voice that sent tingles through a nightclub owner who happened to be listening. He hired her and soon she was being billed as "Evie Symington, the Society Singer."

Stuart Symington by this time was gaining a sizable reputation as an industrial troubleshooter who could take an ailing business, reorganize it, expand its manufacturing and orders and turn it into a thumping moneymaker.

In 1938 in St. Louis the Emerson Electric Manufacturing Company, a small business, was having a bad time struggling through the depression. To make its plight more depressing, it was beset by labor troubles. Emerson got wind of this business magician in the East and lured him with an offer of $24,000 a year salary plus an option of 75,000 shares of stock.

So it was that Stuart Symington came to St. Louis. Emerson was a dismal prospect. It had not been making money, and it had been closed for fifty-three days by a strike. Right away the newcomer ended the strike by making some generous and unconventional concessions. Some conservative businessmen frowned; he was setting a bad example. Symington spoke the language of these union negotiators, got right to the nub of things, and kept his promises. "He always gave us a fair shake without doing us any favors," said one union boss. Labor was impressed and ever after was friendly to him.

Symington reorganized and revitalized Emerson, took it into some new kinds of production, and was looking for other ways to expand its manufacturing when World War II came along. This was to shape a second big change in his life.

Emerson picked up some small military contracts and began paying dividends for the first time in years. The government contracted to erect a $15,000,000 turret plant, and Emerson climbed toward the big money.

The war was over. And so was the industrial career of Stuart Symington. At forty-four he was about to begin a new career in Washington as a top government official.

In what was then believed to be a peaceful world, the U.S. government had $100 billion worth of surplus war property it had to get off its hands—everything from toothbrushes and shoes to barracks and war plants. The man who had done such an outstanding job of war production at Emerson was asked by President Harry S. Truman to undertake the world's greatest merchandising job. Symington accepted, sold his stock holdings, and quit private business. He became the nation's surplus property administrator.

Less than six months later he accepted an appointment as assistant secretary of war for air. This was familiar ground. He had become well informed on air power while making bomber turrets during the war. When the air force won its long fight for independence from the army, Truman appointed Symington the first secretary of the air force. His goal was to make air power a deterrent to Communist military adventures; his specific program was to build an invincible air armada of intercontinental bombers that could carry the atomic bomb to Russia from bases in the Western Hemisphere, if necessary.

Stuart Symington, the reorganizer and revitalizer of industry and ailing governmental departments, was now becoming President Truman's troubleshooter in Washington. Next he was tagged to pull the Reconstruction Finance Corporation out of trouble. He took over in 1951 as one-man boss and straightened it out.

For some time Symington wanted to return to private life. Now woes were piling up for the Truman administration. Relations between him and the president were less cordial than they had once been. Early in 1952 the Symingtons turned homeward.

With the surge in popularity for Dwight Eisenhower that year, election prospects looked bleak for Democrats. Democratic politicos around St. Louis were worried about Missouri. They needed a strong senatorial candidate to head the state ticket, and there wasn't one in sight. Just then Stuart Symington came home from Washington. Here was the answer to their prayers. When broached concerning his availability as a senatorial candidate in the primary, he sputtered the usual: "I am not a politician and have no political ambitions." But then he thought about it for awhile and changed his mind.

He had support from the start. A good segment of organization Democrats saw the vote appeal of a candidate of his eminence, record, and charm. Businessmen looked favorably on him and so did labor. He won the August primary by 185,000 votes and in the November election trounced Republican Senator James P. Kem, who was seeking a second term. Meanwhile, Eisenhower won the state by 29,000 votes.

Evelyn Symington was back in her old familiar Washington again. Once she had been daughter of a senator. Now she was the wife of one. The Symingtons moved into the old Wadsworth home in Georgetown—a home rich with antiques, oil paintings, and memories.

Few freshmen in Congress rose as fast as Senator Symington. He quickly took an effective part in committee investigations and floor debates, and the prestige of Missouri in the Senate rose to its highest in thirty years.

Symington's long fight for a militarily strong America continued. Early in 1956 he was named chairman of a special Senate subcommittee that investigated America's air power and missile program vis-a-vis Russia's. He won respect when he withheld the report until after the elections so the findings could not be used a political fodder.

When Russia sent up a satellite ahead of the United States in October 1957, Symington called for a special meeting of Congress to take stock of the situation. Congress ordered an investigating committee to find ways of speeding up the nation's "lagging" missile program.

This was a victory for Senator Symington and perhaps a victory for America as well. The persistent legislative efforts of the warning voice of Stuart Symington through the years contributed greatly to the success of the nation as a superpower and brought pride to Symington's supporters in St. Louis.

Senator Stuart Symington died on December 14, 1988.

Morton D. May

1959

THE BAND PLAYED "Meet Me in St. Louis." The mayor braced his foot on the shining stainless steel spade and pushed it into the ground. With commendable know-how, he stooped, regripped the handle and turned over a spadeful of fresh earth.

It was a traditional ceremony—breaking ground for a new project. To those in the group gathered together on the downtown riverfront that day, it was a solemn and deeply moving ceremony.

Most of the battles had been lost during twenty years of discouragement, but the war had been won. The tenacious fight for the $30 million Jefferson National Expansion Memorial had ended victoriously, and this first spadeful of dirt would change the drab and vacant riverfront to a shining gateway commemorating the westward progress of the nation.

By 1959 the revitalizing effect was being felt. The memorial with its museums and its stainless steel arch reaching 630 feet into the sky would not be finished until the mid-1970s, but already plans were being made to erect tall apartment houses and office buildings along the fringe of the riverfront area, as well as a huge stadium with 50,000 seats. Too, a new free bridge would soon span the Mississippi River just south of the memorial, connecting interstate highways.

One of the stalwarts who worked for the memorial with a fierce dedication was the then forty-five-year old president of the May Department Stores Companies, Morton D. ("Buster") May.

He was not so busy shaping a prodigious merchandising career that he could not give time to helping his fellow citizens. This help, always quietly unobtrusive, showed a kindliness and compassion that reached people in all walks of life and crossed the lines of race, creed, and national origin. Though he could have done so, he did not acquit his respon-

sibilities to society merely with a checkbook. He gave generously from his pocket, but he gave more generously from his heart.

May was just a twenty-one-year-old college student in 1935 when the taxpayers voted $7.5 million to pay for the city's share of the cost of the riverfront memorial for which the federal government had pledged to put up another $22.5 million. The project was still languishing ten years later when he returned from World War II and settled down to the life of a business executive. He joined the fight for the memorial.

It was believed that a memorial with an arch designed by Eero Saarinen would bring millions of visitors and would rejuvenate downtown St. Louis, which was slipping backward. In his quiet way, May carried on, making converts, lending his zeal to keeping the project alive, using his considerable influence in its behalf.

Several forces combined within the succeeding years to clear away the obstacles to realization of the riverfront dream. One was a hard-hitting series of articles in the *St. Louis Globe-Democrat* deploring the long delay, which was used effectively in Congress by Senator Stuart Symington. Eventually the money to start the memorial was forthcoming from Washington, and the remaining bottleneck, over relocation of the elevated railroad tracks which marred the site, was resolved. But there would have been no memorial had not May, and those like him, kept the project alive.

At about the same time the magnificent Pope Pius XII Memorial Library planned for the campus of Saint Louis University was in danger of not getting enough funds soon enough. It would cost $4 million dollars and $2.3 million of this was to be raised in the St. Louis area. Edgar E. Rand, International Shoe Company president who headed the local drive, had suddenly died when less than one million had been raised. The campaign came almost to a stop. The Very Reverend Paul C. Reinert, then president of the university, asked May to take over leadership of the drive for this simple reason: "The campaign seemed to be drifting, and I believed this library would be tremendously important to St. Louis."

May threw himself into solicitation of funds, working with his characteristic fervor to get the drive rolling again. He broadened the appeal so that the general public became interested regardless of personal faith, and the money began flowing in.

Also at the same time, several Jewish community centers, old and inadequate, were being left behind by the changing city and shifting population. Plans were developed to build a new center on a 108-acre tract at Lindbergh and Schuetz roads, with a branch at Hanley and Olive

Street roads in University City. The Jewish Community Centers Association called on May, and he again found himself general chairman of a fund campaign.

With a deep sense of responsibility to help provide splendid new recreational and cultural facilities, he undertook the chairmanship of this drive. The larger center was to stress family participation and provide enjoyment by people of all ages. Again it was a job that took much of himself, but was one that would leave a lasting monument to the concern of a man for others.

In his youth May was a Boy Scout, and he returned to the movement as an adult. As chairman of the camp committee a number of years ago, he saw the need for more acreage and space for camp facilities. A plan was conceived and the upshot was the eventual realization of the Beaumont Reservation near Eureka, Missouri, one of the largest Scout reservations in the United States.

For his work, May received the highest Scout award, the Silver Beaver. In 1956 the Big Brother Organization honored him "in recognition of his service to the youth of our community." In the field of civic betterment, Buster May was active in such organizations as Civic Progress, Inc., and Downtown St. Louis, Inc. He was also a member of the Chamber of Commerce of Metropolitan St. Louis.

He gave himself as wholly to fostering good music in the city as he did to other interests. And he felt that the symphony orchestra was the foundation of good music. He wanted St. Louis to have the nation's best orchestra, and to make things pleasant for guest soloists who came to town, he often entertained them in his home.

Buster May was a nationally recognized patron of the arts. His own art collection was outstanding, with emphasis on modern art, notably the German impressionists. So that the public could benefit from his collection, he gave the City Art Museum eighty-two pictures, seventy-three sculptures, and seventy-one examples of decorative arts.

May's forebears were not always wealthy merchant princes. It was his grandfather, David May, who began today's department store empire in 1877. David May had come from Europe years before; he was one of those seeking freedom and opportunity in America. At first a partner in a small dry goods business in Hartford, Indiana, he was advised by a doctor to go to Colorado for an asthmatic condition.

He opened a small store in Leadville. A shrewd businessman, May prospered and later opened what today would be called branch stores in adjacent communities. But after ten years he decided Leadville had no future and located a store in Denver, which became the parent of the future merchandising empire.

In 1893 David May came to St. Louis, then the fourth city of the nation, and opened a store called Famous. Eventually he bought out another store which had a long history here—the William Barr Dry Goods Co. And so Famous-Barr was born. It moved into the newly built Railway Exchange Building in 1913, and the headquarters was switched from Denver to St. Louis.

A new generation came along to take over—Morton J. May, son of the founder David May. Next, Morton's son, Morton D., sat in the head office. Though family wealth, prestige, and influence grew tremendously through the years, the succeeding generations never lost the common touch of the man who opened the wood-and-canvas store on Leadville's dusty streets.

Buster May, grandson of the rugged founder, was born in St. Louis on March 25, 1914. He went to Country Day School, where he developed a strong liking for athletics. He took part in football and baseball and developed an excellent forehand and backhand in tennis. Around the age of ten he joined Boy Scout Troop 186 at Country Day, and this opened an interest that was to last through life and have an impact on his community. He found another lasting interest in photography during his boyhood.

Young May chose to attend Dartmouth College at Hanover, New Hampshire. He was impressed by the fact that it had the attributes of both a large school and a small one, and it had high scholastic standards. Here he gained technical knowledge of photography and became an avid and skilled photographer.

It was time for him to begin learning the family business, so during vacations he made himself useful at the store. In the tradition of the company, he began at the bottom. He became so intrigued by the customers that when he returned to college he took a course in psychology to learn more about people.

While still a student at Dartmouth in 1934, May had a rare opportunity to make a trip to Russia with noted free-lance photographer and travelogist Julian Bryan. He spent three months in the Soviet Union with a camera. The trip set him back a semester at college; with a bachelor of arts degree, he graduated with the class of 1936.

Work began in earnest as he followed in the footsteps of his father and grandfather. He started out as the assistant to several department heads and learned the merchandising business from the ground up. He was transferred to the May operation in Cleveland. Late in 1941 he returned to St. Louis where he became divisional manager of a group of departments.

In May 1942, six months after Pearl Harbor, he received a commission in the navy as a lieutenant, junior grade, and was called to active service. Late in the fall of 1942 he was aboard the carrier *Suwanee* and serving in the South Pacific as a ground officer with a navy fighter squadron. His carrier operated off Guadalcanal during the historic battle for that island.

Eventually a major part of his squadron got malaria, and so did he. In the fall of 1943 the navy sent him home with the remnants of his squadron. He had been given two battle stars and the presidential distinguished unit citation.

May resumed his interrupted business career at Famous-Barr, serving as divisional merchandise manager until 1948. Then the first suburban branch store opened in Clayton and he became its manager. Moving rapidly, in 1950 he was made general manager of the entire Famous-Barr operation. In June 1951 he was elected president of the May Department Stores Company empire. His father, Morton J. May, who had been president for a notable thirty-four years, became chairman of the board.

In 1950 May was married to Mrs. Margie Wolcott Gerow. Gracious and popular, Margie May was also a native St. Louisan. She attended Webster Groves High School and Washington University and also has a strong interest in art.

Buster May was an optimist during the dark days of the riverfront memorial fight and remained an optimist about the future of St. Louis.

"I believe St. Louis is on the threshold of terrific redevelopment," he said. "There is a new spirit, and things will happen in the next few years. I can feel the change in attitude. You must have people living downtown; the area must be populated. The value of the future plaza and riverfront apartments cannot be overestimated. The Mill Creek Valley redevelopment, the new riverfront memorial, the stadium, the express highways—all are tremendously important to the future of downtown."

Morton D. May died on April 13, 1983.

Thomas B. Curtis

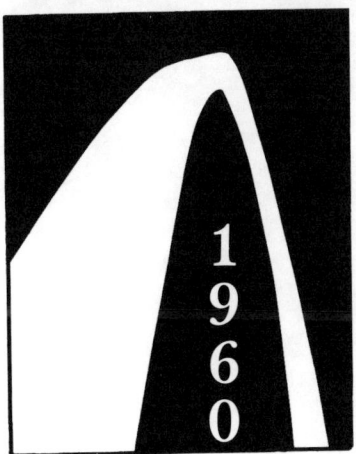

IT WAS PAST SEVEN O'CLOCK on the evening of election day. The polls had closed and the votes were being counted. No one was more interested in the results of that election than Congressman Thomas B. Curtis.

Stocky, combative Curtis had represented the district's citizens in Washington for ten years and had heeded the personal problems of thousands of them. His wife, Susan, and his four sons—his daughter was away at college—wandered in and joined him around the television screen.

Now, in the privacy of his home with only his family near, he heard what the people had to say about him and about sending him back to Washington for another two years. For many years Curtis had formed his own judgments of what was in the best interests of the nation and his constituency. He had stuck to them courageously, even though they sometimes put him on the unpopular side.

It had been a lonesome road politically. For the past four years he had been the only Missouri Republican in Congress. And soon perhaps there wouldn't be any. The Democratic residents of his own district had been increasing steadily, and at each election his majority had diminished.

Suddenly he realized the outcome was of no great concern to him. He had done his job as he saw it, and now it was up to the people whether they wanted him or not.

They did want him. There was never any doubt of it. The televised returns he was watching with his family showed early that he was running way ahead. Tom Curtis was reelected to a sixth term in Congress.

At the sacrifice of much of his private life, the congressman from St. Louis County campaigned for his idea of sound government and, with original thinking, contributed substantially to the processes of Congress.

In his legislative proposals, in his votes on the floor of the House, and in his other official activities, he worked tenaciously for fiscal responsibility and for a solid economy as a basis for national greatness.

Congressman Curtis left his mark on innumerable bills and legislative acts that affected national life, but at the same time, few congressmen gave so much attention to the needs of their home communities. He did not center his efforts on his own district, but worked just as hard for the betterment of the greater St. Louis area and indeed of the entire state.

He played a large part in obtaining for St. Louis a $133 million flood control project, although the specific benefits largely accrued to two other congressional districts represented by Democrats. He was a stalwart in the fight to get rolling and keep rolling, through continued federal appropriations, the Jefferson National Expansion Memorial on the riverfront. And he was chief expediter in bringing about local and federal cooperation and in clearing the way for the erection of six thirteen-story apartments on Memorial Plaza.

Partly due to his work in Washington were the new Federal Office Building for St. Louis and the Federal Records Center for the county. Congressman Curtis also sponsored a resolution which provided federal funds for a restudy of the flood control needs of the controversial and lagging Meramec River Basin, and was successful in helping St. Louis County purchase at a reasonable price 232 acres of land at Jefferson Barracks for a park.

Tom Curtis was a member of the "economic bloc" in Congress and as such stood for conservative fiscal policies. He was dubious of "big spending" by government as the way to national growth. He favored a balanced budget, believing that deficit spending and fiscal irresponsibility could lead only to harmful inflation, "which is nothing more than another insidious tax on the people." He was zealous on behalf of the free enterprise system and believed in strong anti-trust provisions and a free and active labor movement.

Congressman Curtis said he was a good friend of union members and all of his legislative activities were for their benefit. He sought to free them from irresponsible, dishonest, and dictatorial bosses who harmed unions.

The National Committee for an Effective Congress, a non-partisan organization, twice endorsed him as one of the outstanding members of Congress because of his "constructive leadership" and his "potential for future leadership."

Thomas Bradford Curtis was born in Webster Groves on May 14,

1911, the second of a family of six children, one of whom died in infancy. There was a tradition of law in the family. Tom's grandfather, William Curtis, had been an attorney and for twenty-five years was dean of Washington University Law School. His father had been a prominent lawyer, too.

After graduating from high school, Tom went to Dartmouth College at Hanover, New Hampshire, and one of the proudest developments of his life came of that. He became a member of the board of trustees at his alma mater. There, too, he came to know such schoolmates as Nelson Rockefeller, former governor of New York, and Meade Alcorn, who became the Republican Party national chairman.

Young Tom was a sturdy fellow with athletic ability who was kept off the Dartmouth football team by an ill-timed appendectomy. He later turned to soccer, earning a letter, and was the team's top scorer. Scholastically he did so well that he graduated with honors.

Despite the family legal tradition, he toyed with the idea of becoming an engineer. He had a bent for mathematics and the physical sciences. But he soon discovered he was even more interested in social sciences. He was attracted to humanity and its problems and finally concluded that a lawyer had a good vantage point from which to work within the vast human laboratory.

With his A.B. degree from Dartmouth under his arm, he entered Washington University Law School. He graduated in 1935, but before he settled down to briefs and clients, he took a bicycle tour through Europe.

When Tom Curtis started thinking seriously about political affiliation, he turned to the Republican Party. From the start he took a lively interest in party politics, became a member of the John Marshall Club, and before long was president of St. Louis County's Young Republicans. He became ambitious in 1936 and stubbed his toe when he ran for the Republican nomination for state representative. He was then young, unknown, and, he added, "I think I had trouble convincing voters I wasn't a Democrat, because of my father and grandfather [who were]."

In the half-dozen years before World War II, Curtis was busy in the law. He worked in many ways for the public interest, becoming active in the St. Louis Bar Association. His varied interests embraced the American Red Cross, the Community Chest, the Big Brothers Organization, the Visiting Nurses Association, and the Boy Scouts.

In 1940 Tom's father died and Tom formed a new firm, Biggs, Hensley, Curtis & Biggs. That same year he married Susan Ross Chivvis, a member of an old St. Louis family that numbered among its forebears

William Carr Lane, the city's first mayor. The new Mrs. Curtis was a graduate of Mary Institute and Washington University.

In March 1942 Governor Forrest Donnell appointed Tom Curtis a member of the St. Louis County Board of Election Commissioners. He served only a month. The nation was at war with Japan. He enlisted and served in the Naval Air Corps for three years with distinction, leaving as a lieutenant commander. He received the commendation and citation ribbon, the Philippine Liberation ribbon, and the Pacific and Atlantic Theater ribbons.

He resumed his law practice and his interest in politics after the war. He became the Republican committeeman for Gravois Township and in 1950, after a stirring experience as eastern Missouri campaign manager for Robert Taft, who was then seeking the Republican presidential nomination, decided to throw his hat in the ring again.

He ran for Congress in the old Twelfth Congressional District and won by about 4,000 votes. Two years later, with boundary lines redrawn to form the new Second District, he won again and then repeated the victory every two years, even though the district was steadily filling up with Democrats.

In Washington, many of the 435 congressmen had their headquarters in the old House Office Building, a large, oblong stone structure a few blocks from the Capitol. At night almost all the offices were dark, but at least several nights a week the tall window of one of them was lighted. The solitary worker behind it was Tom Curtis.

Among the few mementos in his Washington office was a rock about as large as a medium-sized potato. One night he saw teen-aged hoodlums attacking visitors to the Capitol. Highly incensed, he moved forward to the rescue and was met with a barrage of stones. When the melee was over and his anger had cooled, he pocketed one of the stones that had been shied at him and took it home as a souvenir.

Curtis had a bulldog courage and tenacity in pushing legislation he thought was right. It sometimes paid off, he observed, for the unpopular issues of today may become the popular issues of year after next and be enacted into law.

The years showed him to be an able, articulate debater on the floor—he loved a good argument—and a razor-sharp interrogator. He was a stickler for procedure because he believed it protected people's rights.

Curtis was a year-round congressman. He or his staff were available to constituents and any other callers or letter-writers through the twelve months in both Washington and his district headquarters in Clayton. In a normal year, Curtis lived about eight months in Washington and four months at home. When at home he spent over half his time on congressional chores and less than half at his law office.

"Why am I a congressman?" he mused. "Sometimes I wonder myself."

But he didn't wonder long, and his answer was uncomplicated.

"I find it interesting work. You work and work and lose and lose. And just when you are down about it, something happens and you win."

August A. Busch, Jr.

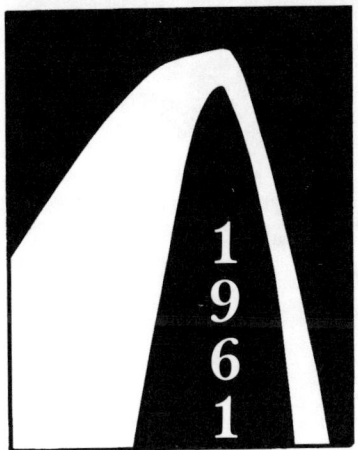

IN AN AGE OF STREAMLINED GLASS AND STEEL buildings, August A. Busch, Jr., sat at a rolltop desk in a high-ceilinged room of what was once an old red brick schoolhouse.

From this office, which once had blackboards on the walls and rows of children droning their lessons, the ruler of Anheuser-Busch, Inc., ran the world's largest brewing empire.

In an age of small homes, Gussie Busch lived in a baronial thirty-four-room French Renaissance mansion with furnishings to match. And in the age of the jet plane and racing car, he could be seen on a pleasant weekend driving a coach behind four spanking bays over his 281-acre estate, waving at passing motorists and looking for all the world like a country squire who just dropped in from the nineteenth century.

While August Anheuser Busch, Jr., may have had a sentimental feeling for the history and traditions of his century-old brewing family and for the gracious life of the past, he was a very modern businessman whose huge and aggressively competitive company was in the forefront of the brewing industry.

He also had a fierce pride in St. Louis and a zeal to make it a better place to live. He worked hard and courageously in behalf of the community, using not only his own time and money, but the resources of giant Anheuser-Busch, Inc., which he headed as president and chairman of the board.

Twice when the community was threatened with loss, Gussie and his company stepped up and saved the day—once when the city almost lost its beloved baseball Cardinals and again when it almost lost the new sports stadium, which did much to rejuvenate downtown St. Louis.

And when Saint Louis University needed someone to head an appeal

for emergency funds to meet the rapidly expanding educational needs of the community, it turned to him. The campaign was so successful that more than two-thirds of the fund was raised in much less than half the time allotted.

Gussie Busch was a man of tolerance, consideration, and good will. He stood up for his convictions, political or otherwise. A scion of generations of wealth, he never lost the common touch; nor did he soften up.

In 1953 the St. Louis Cardinals were about to be sold to another city when Gussie Busch and the Anheuser-Busch brewery galloped to the rescue. When no other St. Louisans with money seemed interested in saving the ball club for St. Louis, the brewery bought it for $3.75 million, and Gussie, in addition to his other responsibilities, took over the presidency of the team. The brewery then bought Sportsmans Park, changed its name to Busch Stadium and at much expense rehabilitated it into the best-looking old park in baseball. When a new stadium was needed downtown, Anheuser-Busch again saved the day by putting up $5 million of the $20 million needed.

During Busch's presidency, Anheuser-Busch gave about $500,000 to Washington University, which built a biological laboratory named in honor of his grandfather, Adolphus Busch. A new student center erected on the campus of Saint Louis University also bears the Busch name in memory of Adolphus and his grandson, Adolphus III.

One of the many awards Gussie Busch received for public service was the President's Patriotic Service Award, the highest given to a civilian. It was presented to him by the department of defense for his service as chairman of Armed Forces Week. He received also the Fleur-de-Lis Award from Saint Louis University, the highest honor it gives to a lay person.

Busch believed that every citizen should strive for good government by taking an interest in politics. He set an example in presidential elections. In 1960, when many businessmen were running for cover because of the touchy issues involved, he came out forthrightly for Democrat John F. Kennedy and was chairman of the St. Louis fund-raising dinner.

In itself, Anheuser-Busch has been an invaluable asset to St. Louis. Its beer has carried the name of the city all over the nation and around the world. It has kept St. Louis at or near the top in the industry and has shown, by its tremendous success, that this city is a good place to do business.

Another asset to the community has been the estate that surrounds the spacious home of Gussie Busch on Gravois road south of the city. It has the finest deer park anywhere and contains a variety of exotic animals. Its *Bauernhof*, or German farmstead, is out of an Old World picture book. There, too, is the cabin in which Ulysses S. Grant lived during his years of failure just prior to the Civil War.

Anheuser-Busch got its start in 1857, when a new arrival from Germany came to St. Louis, eighteen-year-old Adolphus Busch. During the next eight years he found his bearings in the new land, married Lilly Anheuser, served with the Union Army in the Civil War, and was given charge in 1865 of the faltering brewery that had fallen into his father-in-law's hands.

Adolphus Busch was a man of action and imagination, a hale and hearty fellow with a loud, lusty voice, one who made friends easily. He was a supersalesman, and a business genius. The languishing brewery perked up under his ministrations and began flourishing. By the turn of the century, the Anheuser-Busch Brewing Association (Anheuser died in 1880) was turning out one million barrels of beer a year and leading all other American breweries. Budweiser, a light lager beer, had been developed in 1876 and had walked away with top awards in international expositions.

Adolphus Busch, a striking figure with twirled mustache and goatee, was a titan among brewers and had become a legend before he died in Germany in 1913 at the age of seventy-six. With the death of Adolphus Busch, the sun sank on a golden era. Europe burst into the flames of World War I. Shortly afterward, Prohibition began in the United States. A long, dark night settled down on the brewing industry. Most breweries quit doing business, but August A. Busch, Sr., the dynamic son of Adolphus, fought for survival. At his side were his two sons, Adolphus III, the elder, and August, Jr. They turned to the manufacture of nonbeer products, such as yeast, corn, and malt syrups, trying to make a living.

It was a long pull, but father, sons, and brewery held together until the dawn of repeal came up like thunder at 12:01 A.M. April 7, 1933. In St. Louis thousands of factory whistles welcomed the return of beer, and fleets of laden brewery trucks rolled through the streets.

In 1934 August A. Busch, Sr., died. He was succeeded by Adolphus III. The younger Gussie, who had risen through the ranks, carried on at his side as first vice-president and general manager.

After repeal Budweiser was again the most popular beer in America, and Anheuser-Busch resumed its comfortable position of leadership until 1945. When World War II came, Gussie, then forty-three, joined the army ordnance department. He ended his service three years later with the rank of colonel and was given the Legion of Merit for notable service in bringing about cooperation between industry and the military.

While in the service he turned down a plea to become a candidate for mayor of St. Louis with a forthright statement that he believed he could best serve his city and nation by continuing to fight the war.

In 1946 Adolphus Busch III died of cancer at age fifty-five. August A. Busch, Jr., became president. He was forty-seven.

A strong man was needed at the company's helm. The complacency of Anheuser-Busch as the world's leading brewery had just been shattered. Hustling Milwaukee brewers had taken the lead. In 1946 Pabst barely nosed out Busch; in 1947 Schlitz announced that it was the biggest beer seller in America. Anheuser-Busch was stunned when it dropped not to second place, but to fourth.

Gussie Busch brought the company a dynamic aggressive leadership. "More like his grandfather Adolphus every day," observed one of the older executives. The elder statesmen of the company began to respect his judgment.

To win back the leadership in beer, Anheuser-Busch had to expand. Gussie preached to everyone who would listen. He shouted. He pounded tables at conferences. His conservative opponents eventually gave up. He kicked off a $50 million expansion program and started work on a $34 million brewery in Newark, New Jersey. A couple of years later, a $25 million brewery at Los Angeles began rising, and a third one, costing $25 million, was built at Tampa, Florida, along with the famed Busch Gardens.

Expansion and imaginative salesmanship paid off. In 1953 Anheuser-Busch recaptured the lead with an all-time record of 6,711,222 barrels.

The first thing Gussie learned when Anheuser-Busch bought the Cardinals was that he couldn't buy a pennant. "Baseball is a son-of-a-gun business," he said—he who had licked giants and dragons in the beer business. "They call it a sport, but it's really a tough business.

"My ambition is to get a championship baseball team for St. Louis before I die. Something to go with that new stadium and new riverfront memorial and new Mill Creek Valley development that are going to make St. Louis the kind of city it should be."

August A. Busch, Jr., died on September 29, 1989.

Edwin M. Clark

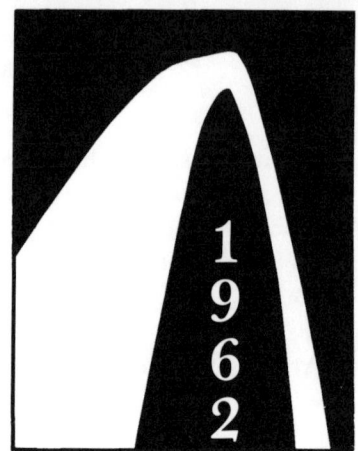

A DC-3 THAT HAD BUCKED A HOWLING HEADWIND all the way from Philadelphia swung low across the Mississippi River and eased down onto Lambert Field. Its wheels touched the runway and rolled to a stop in a slashing rain that blurred the landing lights.

Out of the blustery rainstorm and into the late-night loneliness of the airport terminal stepped Edwin M. Clark. He had just been transferred from Philadelphia to St. Louis to become the vice-president of operations for the Southwestern Bell Telephone Company. Briefcase in hand, pipe in mouth, he was getting his first look at St. Louis, his future home.

That was in 1950. For a while he knew hardly a soul, and there was no nod of recognition from those who passed him on the street. But seldom had a stranger become so quickly a useful part of his new community, and seldom had anyone contributed so much to its civic progress in so short a time.

Clark was blunt, direct, and impatient with failure, and it was soon evident he was a man who got things done. In fifteen months he was elected president of Southwestern Bell, which spread its cables over five and one-half states and was one of the largest operating branches of the Bell system.

Quickly the people of the St. Louis area became aware that Ed Clark was not only an unusual business executive, but a generous citizen who earnestly believed it was his responsibility to give at least ten percent of his time and energy for the betterment of his community. It was clear also that he had the drive, forcefulness, and determination to accomplish what he wanted.

His dynamics as a civic leader were fully revealed when he was drafted

by the chamber of commerce in 1952-53 to head a committee whose task was to find a remedy for the postwar swell of traffic congestion that was strangling downtown St. Louis. Clark and his committee came up with a jolting master traffic control plan that was an effective palliative if not a cure.

From then on the services of Ed Clark—a large-shouldered former football end for Virginia Military Institute—as a civic leader were constantly in demand, and he responded far above and beyond the call of duty.

Through the years he fought in the forefront for bond issues to bring new public improvements. He headed various civic enterprises and worked with several groups dedicated to community progress. Like all men of sound judgment who look to the future, he had a zeal for preparing youth for the citizenship and leadership of tomorrow. Much of his effort was in the Boy Scout movement.

As president of the United Fund of Greater St. Louis, he organized, supervised, and gave unprecedented impetus to a record-breaking campaign. It was the first time in forty years of federated fund raising that a goal was reached in the scheduled thirty days.

At the request of Governor John Dalton, Clark served as chairman of Missourians for Progress, the group that spearheaded the successful campaign for a state constitutional amendment which permanently increased the state gasoline tax for road improvements.

Finally, he shouldered the burden of leadership in a new effort to solve, through a form of public ownership, the mass transportation mess in the greater St. Louis area. Negotiations set up a unified area transit system under the control of the Bi-State Development Agency. The Public Service Company and thirteen other private lines were to be purchased with bonds floated to pay the cost.

Being a public utility man himself, Clark brought an invaluable special knowledge to the Bi-State negotiations to acquire the fifteen bus and streetcar lines of the St. Louis area, on both sides of the Mississippi, and weld them into one big unified transit system.

St. Louisans liked the way Ed Clark handled the traffic problem in 1953, so that same year Mayor Raymond R. Tucker asked him to head a committee of 100 to lead the fight for passage of a bond issue to create a three-block parkway between Memorial and Aloe plazas and set up an area for seven downtown apartment houses, now known as the Plaza Apartments.

He received the St. Louis Award for the master control plan and his effective guidance of the bond issue, a remarkable achievement for a citizen who had lived in the community about three years.

"St. Louis needs more men like you," Mayor Tucker said at the presentation ceremony.

Although a St. Louis County resident who would be subject to the tax, Clark played a key role in the successful 1954 campaign that passed a city charter amendment giving the city of St. Louis the power to levy its own earnings tax. The tax rescued the municipal government from imminent fiscal disaster and drastic curtailment of its functions and services.

The business career of Edwin M. Clark was centered in his walnut-paneled office on the top floor of the pyramidal twenty-six-story stone telephone building at Tenth and Pine streets. From this office, he directed a company whose poles, wires, and telephones, covered half of Illinois and the states of Missouri, Kansas, Arkansas, Oklahoma, and Texas—a territory comprising about one-tenth of the United States. With 55,000 employees, it was one of the largest of the Bell system's twenty-three operating companies.

In 1962 St. Louis had not kept pace with some of the nation's more progressive cities, but Ed Clark believed it was a mistake to criticize instead of boost the community. Many things were needed to be done, and some of his goals were these: to eliminate tolls from the Mississippi bridges and make them as free as the streets; to set up joint metropolitan districts for police, fire, health, and penal systems; and to create one or more industrial parks with all the necessary inducements to bring in more industry.

Clark was a member of the board of Civic Progress, Inc., and was its president for two years. He belonged to Downtown St. Louis, Inc., and was co-chairman for the Citizens Committee for City-County Cooperation. He served two terms as president of the St. Louis Area Council Boy Scouts of America.

A measure of his activities could be gained from a list of the boards of directors on which he served. They included those of the Mercantile Trust Company, Transit Casualty Company, Automobile Club of Missouri, and the Municipal Opera. He was a trustee of Westminster College at Fulton, Missouri, and on the advisory council of Saint Louis University. He belonged to the Noonday, Racquet, Bogey, and Bellerive country clubs. He was also a trustee of Central Presbyterian Church and on its board of deacons.

Edwin M. Clark was born at the turn of the century in Danville, Virginia, but his booming voice had little regional overtone. He was the second of seven children, and his father was a locomotive engineer on the Southern Railroad. With so many children in the family, money was scarce around the Clark home when Edwin was a boy, so he earned $1.50 a week—not a bad sum in those days—by getting up at 4:15 A.M. daily and delivering the morning paper.

He liked sports and was a good athlete when young. Football was his specialty. During summers, he worked in the textile mills and, wanting no part of the miserable life of the millworker, he decided to go to college and prepare himself for better things. He chose Virginia Military Institute at Lexington—where Stonewall Jackson taught for the ten years preceding the Civil War—and borrowed the necessary money from a Danville bank. He later repaid it at the rate of five dollars a week.

Clark got a degree in electrical engineering and made a name for himself as an end on the football team, which beat the formidable University of Pennsylvania for the first time in many years. To fulfill an obligation, after graduation he taught mathematics and coached the football team for a year at Augusta Military Academy. The year over, he got a thirty-dollar-a-week job with Western Electric, a manufacturing unit of the Bell system in New York City.

After a year of installing dial telephone equipment in New York offices, he decided he could never like that city. On the way back to Virginia, he got a job with Pennsylvania Bell Telephone Company from a fellow who saw the VMI-Pennsylvania game and was soon a district engineer.

After getting married in 1927, he and his new wife, the former Eleanor McKay, moved about Pennsylvania for the telephone company with sojourns of various lengths at Greensburg, Carnegie, Pittsburgh, and Philadelphia. The direction of able, hard-working Ed Clark was upward. He climbed steadily through the ranks until he approached the top where, he once told a group of students, "the competitors are fewer, but they can run faster." In 1941 he was made vice-president of personnel and in 1949 became vice-president of operations.

In 1950 Clark was offered the job of vice-president of operations with Southwestern Bell. It was the same job he already held with the Pennsylvania company, but it offered more money and more opportunity. Though he had never seen St. Louis, he accepted and made the stormy plane journey that introduced him to the city.

His job as president of Southwestern Bell was challenging. For him there was no forty-hour week. Most of the time he put in from sixty to eighty hours, and about one-fourth of his time was spent traveling over the vast domain his company covered. He liked to see for himself what was going on. With such a heavy business schedule he still found time to make St. Louis a better community in which to live, to do business, and to rear children.

Clark gave much to St. Louis. Those who knew Edwin M. Clark say that he gave far more than ten percent of his time. But that was only part of his contribution. His earnest labors in behalf of the public interest invigorated the whole community and stimulated greater effort.

Edwin M. Clark died on February 12, 1978.

Paul C. Reinert

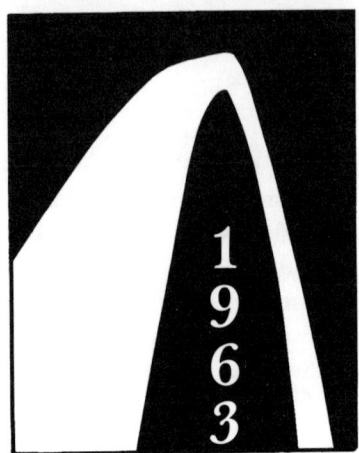

IT WAS NOT OFTEN that Father Paul C. Reinert, S.J., president of Saint Louis University, had time to look out a window. But when he did occasionally get up from his horseshoe-shaped desk in venerable DuBourg Hall and walk over to the nearest arched window, he saw no grassy campus with stately trees, but a bustling city. Less than fifty feet from his office window was a turgid stream of traffic, making its noisy way along Grand Boulevard.

Reinert's was an urban university in the midtown heart of St. Louis, a university whose halls of learning mingled with the streets and buildings of the surrounding city. That was the way the Very Reverend Paul Reinert preferred it to be. Ever since he became president of the university in 1949, he had been in the forefront of those favoring a closer relationship between the urban university and its community. Under his leadership, Saint Louis University shed its aloofness and took a larger and more intimate role in vital community matters. The traditional separation of "town and gown" disappeared from the noted Jesuit institution.

Father Reinert, whose tremendous energy amazed and sometime alarmed those who knew him well, managed to find time from his tasks as head of a great university to become one of the community's leaders in civic progress and in striving for interracial equality and the betterment of other human relationships.

When Father Reinert looked out his window on the main floor of mellow, gable-roofed DuBourg Hall in 1963, he could see more than the traffic on Grand Boulevard a few feet away. A new crop of university buildings was also visible, the result of a five-year expansion development campaign. The new school structures made a greater university

and a greater St. Louis, because they meant that the university had committed itself to staying in midtown.

As president of the university, Reinert had much to do with its decision to stay in the city. He was the heart of the expansion enterprise from the inception of the breathtaking plan to its completion, taking on the long, arduous, and masterly job of salesmanship and scoring a tremendous fund-raising triumph.

Reinert loved St. Louis and became an intimate part of it. He was ever ready to help anyone interested in its improvement. He served with Civic Progress and was one of those who worked hard and effectively to bring educational television station KETC to St. Louis in the early 1950s. His ability as an educator and college administrator made his service sought nationally by educational groups and by two presidents of the United States. And, before all else, he was a spiritual leader—kindly, humble, prayerful. A fellow Jesuit described him as "a man with a deep religious motivation in behalf of mankind."

In 1955 Reinert became a member of the Missouri delegation to the White House Conference on Education, and a year later President Dwight D. Eisenhower appointed him to a thirty-six-man committee on higher education. He was part of a thirteen-man educational advisory committee of the International Cooperation Administration. In 1961 he was called to Washington to discuss the newly established Peace Corps with its director, and the university later trained Peace Corps personnel. He was named to a special committee appointed by the Secretary of Health, Education and Welfare to advise federal officials on all governmental problems relating to higher education. Such was the character of many more calls upon his services by the federal government and by the state of Missouri.

While the prime goal of a university must always be to educate its students and gather knowledge, Father Reinert believed it could and should use some of its abundant resources for the welfare and betterment of the community in which it was located. He was always ready to step out of his academic gown and lend a hand.

In 1963 he was appointed to the newly created St. Louis Research Council, a not-for-profit corporation made up of Saint Louis University, Washington University, and major local industries. It was organized to develop and promote the St. Louis region as a major scientific, educational, and research center.

To perform his manifold duties, as well as his plethora of extracurricular tasks, required time, vigor, and endurance. His reputed eighty-hour work week was no fiction, and some his colleagues felt this frequently mentioned figure was conservative. Nonetheless, he was always calm and relaxed and made other people feel that way.

Despite his heavy schedule, he was a confirmed "do-it-yourselfer." He wrote his own speeches. He typed out articles in the evening. He liked to answer the telephone himself. He penned a surprising number of personal notes, particularly condolences.

A three-letter man in high school, he liked sports, watched Saint Louis University basketball games, and was occasionally seen at St. Louis Cardinals games. Friends remarked upon his good sense of humor and felt it tended to sustain him. Said a fellow Jesuit, "He goes about things gently and quietly, but when some big thing comes along, he sets his chin and come hell or high water he'll see it through."

Another colleague said of him, "The unselfishness of the man is amazing. For all the work he does, for all the money he raises, he doesn't get a dime."

Paul C. Reinert was born August 12, 1910, in Boulder, Colorado. His folks had moved there from a small town in Iowa. Paul was the oldest of six children. The boys were robust, tall, noisy, active, and vigorous. An athletic bunch who liked baseball, football, basketball, and other sports, they were good scholars, too. And good church-goers.

Their mother was devout, and so was the grandfather, who went to church every day, served Mass, and sang in the choir. He built a wooden altar for the boys in their home, and one of their childhood games was to play at celebrating Mass. Just across the street from their home was the Sacred Heart Church and school, which they attended. When Father Reinert returned to his home town to dedicate a new Sacred Heart Church, he found that his old family home had become the pastor's residence.

After young Paul finished Sacred Heart Elementary School, he was confronted with the fact that there was no Catholic high school in Boulder. So he was sent to Denver to attend Regis High School. There he became acquainted with the Jesuits who ran the school.

Young Paul Reinert made his mark as a good scholar and an excellent athlete. As he grew older and pondered a career, his mind most often turned toward law. But near the end of his last year at Regis there came a sudden change in his plans and in his whole life. It was the spring before his graduation from high school and the time of the annual religious retreat. The retreat was conducted by Father Francis J. O'Hern, S.J., who happened to be from Saint Louis University. During that retreat, Paul's heart turned toward God and he knew that he wanted to go into a teaching order.

"A classmate of mine and I decided we would go in together," Father Reinert recalls. "We were close friends; we both played on the football team. He was center and I was guard." Reinert's friend became Father Daniel Campbell, who taught at Saint Louis University High School.

In the fall of 1927, Reinert entered the Jesuit order at St. Stanislaus Seminary in Florissant and began the long and rigorous education every Jesuit undergoes. He spent four years at St. Stanislaus and then three years at Saint Louis University, receiving his bachelor's degree in 1933 and his master's degree in 1934. He was ordained at St. Mary's College at St. Mary's, Kansas, in 1940, and received in Licentiate in Sacred Theology in 1941. He taught at Creighton University High School in Omaha and was registrar and teacher at St. Mary's College. Then he attended Chicago University, where he studied educational administration and received his Ph.D. in 1944. (In due time the four younger brothers of Paul Reinert went to Regis. Two followed him into the Jesuit order.)

Paul Reinert's next stop was to be Saint Louis University. He arrived in September 1944 to take the post of assistant dean of the College of Arts and Sciences. Upon his arrival, young and inexperienced Father Reinert, who was then thirty-four, found a great surprise. The dean he was to assist had been transferred. Father Reinert was made the new dean.

"I had no experience and there was no one to teach me," he recalled. "It was probably a profitable experience in the long run, but at the time it was frightening."

World War II ended the next year and the university and its young dean were thrown into a welter of problems. Returning veterans under the GI bill swelled the university to bursting. Quonset huts were set up as classrooms on the campus. The world was changing politically, economically, and socially. So was university administration. The old methods of education were obsolete. As the university began retooling for the new age, young Father Reinert was in on the ground floor.

In 1948 he moved up. He was named executive vice-president of the university, a newly created office. He became advisor to the president and active in the administration. And then the president, the Reverend Patrick J. Halloran, was stricken by a heart attack. In January 1949 Father Paul C. Reinert became the twenty-sixth president of Saint Louis University.

From the start of his presidency, Father Reinert began bringing the best brains, specialized knowledge, and resources of the community and university together for the benefit of both. Early he created a president's council of prominent business and civic leaders to advice the university and then a similar women's advisory council.

The soaring enrollments, the need to maintain educational quality, and the squeeze of inflation caused him to turn much of his time and thought to raising money. After several years of planning, the university came up with a breathtaking ten-year expansion development plan timed to end in 1968, the school's 150th anniversary. Even Father Reinert was frightened at the goals, but they were achieved, eight months ahead of schedule. By the close of that year, Reinert's administration had brought the university to national stature and local acclaim.

H. Sam Priest

With the end of World War II and the start of the atomic age came a great explosion of crime in the United States, especially in its congested cities. Organized racketeers muscled in where they could. Hoodlums slugged and mugged. Juvenile gangs roamed. Murder, robbery, assault, auto theft, and all the other outrages against the life and property of peaceful citizens increased appallingly until the rate of the crime explosion outstripped the population explosion by five to one. And then in 1963 the most shocking of crimes occurred when President John F. Kennedy was shot down in public with a mail-order rifle.

To no one in St. Louis was this long-continuing and ever-growing crime wave of more concern than to H. Sam Priest. And no one did more about it. Sam Priest was president of the St. Louis Board of Police Commissioners, a powerful team of four citizens appointed by the governor of Missouri to run the state-controlled St. Louis Police Department

The Priest board carried out a comprehensive program of reorganization which improved and modernized almost every phase of police operation, giving it efficiency, quality, and honesty. The St. Louis Police Department in 1964 was unquestionably one of the best in the United States because of the enlightened and progressive advancements made under Priest's leadership.

It proved that statement by firmly holding the line against the ugly upsurge of crime that almost overwhelmed American law and order. The annual uniform crime reports of the FBI showed that the city's crime rate was kept well below the national average. It also was kept very much lower than the average crime rate of other large cities in the United States.

The efficiency of the taut, streamlined, modernized St. Louis police system was so superior during the Sam Priest regime that it even kept

the crime rate in this community substantially under that of cities with relatively more manpower. Over a period of years, the twenty other large cities of the nation increased the size of their police forces an average of twenty-five percent. St. Louis in the same period, while keeping its crime rate much lower, decreased its manpower nearly three percent.

The police were extensively motorized in conformance with the best modern police practice, and this raised the effectiveness of the force. Making a dishonest living became more difficult and hazardous for the criminal. Another salient move by the Sam Priest board was the strategic concentration of the greatest amount of police manpower at the time and place of most prevalent crime.

In the sweeping reorganization which began in 1957, energetic Sam Priest and his board not only transformed and modernized the police department operation and facilities, but also remodeled the six-story police headquarters building erected in 1927. Improvements ranged from a decoy squad to one of the finest systems of police radio communications. New ideas ranged from an uncomplicated canine corps, copied from London, to an electronic computer center which revolutionized some phases of police work. St. Louis pioneered in the application of the computer to law enforcement, and progressive police forces all over the nation watched the department's accomplishments in this new field.

Priest was an incorruptible police administrator. Though once a politician himself, he resisted all political pressures while president of the board. He made the police force a rampart against the invasion of St. Louis by gamblers, underworld racketeers, and organized crime in any form. He drove off any who wanted to weaken law enforcement or undermine police discipline. He demanded honesty of the police and sought men of high quality and good principles for its ranks.

One of his first acts in 1946 was to install the FBI system of uniform reports and records, which stopped a common but deplorable police practice of destroying, concealing, delaying, or "downgrading" crime reports to hide the true crime picture to make a district or department look better than it was. In 1964 St. Louis had the only police force whose crime reports were checked and audited by an independent organization, the Governmental Research Institute.

Priest often said he wanted to see St. Louis with "a police department that would not win a popularity contest, but that would do its job well and win the respect of the people." Another of his early acts was to establish the noted Police Academy, revamped and enlarged to meet the complex schooling needs of a modern force. The ability to read and write was enough to be a policeman at one time, but in 1964 a high school education was a minimum requirement. Intelligence tests then showed that police recruits were above average.

Though the police board, competing with private industry for high class employees, had difficulty filling its manpower quota with men of this standard at the somewhat low police pay, Priest considered abhorrent any notion of lowering the standards to fill the vacancies. Rather, his board fought tenaciously to get the legislature to raise pay, got two increases totaling thirty-five percent and sought a third.

Research was the greatest contribution Sam Priest made to police work, many police administrators believed. To bring the best to the St. Louis department, he sought the aid and advice of experts and specialists all over the world and leaned heavily on the Governmental Research Institute.

Henry Samuel Priest II was born in St. Louis on January 14, 1906, the son of prominent lawyer George T. Priest, who was himself at one time a member of the St. Louis police board. He was named after his grandfather, Judge Henry S. Priest, a well-known federal jurist of a generation ago whose favorite aversions were the Ku Klux Klan and Prohibition, both of which flourished in his day.

Young Sam Priest, whose mother, Mabel Priest, died when he was seven, grew up in the tradition of law and politics, both of which he heard discussed with gusto around the dinner table. After public school he went to the old Smith Academy and then to Western Military Academy at Alton, Illinois.

As he grew up, he had no inclination to follow in paternal footsteps and become a lawyer, but politics fascinated him. His hero was William L. Igoe, a close friend of the family and the big man in Democratic politics here.

When it came time to face the world, young Sam Priest wasn't sure what he wanted to do. After several jobs he settled down as a clerk in a St. Louis stockbroker's office and was thinking seriously of making a career of stocks and bonds, when along came the crash of 1929 and knocked the stock market flat, together with his aspirations.

As a bewildered young man, he watched the Great Depression stalk the land like an economic plague. He wondered why this had happened to America, and he thought he might help do something about it by interesting himself in politics and government.

He joined the Jefferson Club. He mixed with the young folks in politics and became president of the Young Democratic Club. In 1932 and 1933 he campaigned for Francis Wilson for governor (he died before the election), Franklin D. Roosevelt for president, and Bernard F. Dickmann for mayor.

Mayor Dickmann made Sam Priest the secretary of the city's important Public Welfare Department. Priest was affable, energetic, capable, and had a definite flair for politics. In 1934 he ran for office himself. He was elected clerk of the circuit court, a job which had been clutched tightly for many years by a Republican. Priest moved across Twelfth and Market from the city hall to the tall new civil courts building. At twenty-eight he was the youngest man ever elected circuit clerk and at that time the youngest holding any elective office in St. Louis.

He rolled up his sleeves and piled into the unkempt operation. With his chief deputy, Alfred Fleishman (later of Fleishman-Hillard public relations counselors) and his staff, he put in 4,000 hours of overtime, at night and without pay, to bring order out of chaos during the summer of 1935. He brought modern business methods to his office, installed an efficient new central filing system, put an abrupt end to political, racial, religious, or any other kind of favoritism, and in his spare time collected $250,000 in delinquent court costs that long ago had been given up for lost.

His transformation of the circuit clerk's office attracted wide attention. Those who scrutinized the remarkable young fellow who was making a name for himself in politics discovered that he was not a radical reformer, but a quiet clear-headed organizer who was alert to new ideas and who believed in bringing practical, efficient, and modern business methods to public office.

A contemporary president of the American Bar Association wrote to him, "I wish there were a thousand clerks like you. What progress we could make then."

The circuit clerk's office was his for as long as he wanted it. A petition expressing appreciation of his service was signed by 1,200 lawyers of both parties. He was elected handily to a second term in 1938 and to a third in 1942, although a resurgent Republican party was then sweeping nearly all other Democrats out of office.

During World War II, Sam Priest found time to serve with the Missouri State Guard, whose business and filing methods he overhauled. He was advanced to colonel and this led to an important change in his life.

A man of such remarkable business and organizing talent could not escape the eye of private industry, and Gen. Clifford W. Gaylord, then the adjutant-general of Missouri, had plenty of opportunity to get a close look at him. After the war, and with his third term not completed, Sam Priest resigned as circuit clerk to become vice-president and member of the board of the Gaylord Container Corporation.

Out of the capricious game of politics, his interest in good government and the public welfare did not diminish, but became solid and deep. In 1946 Mark Eagleton, then president of the St. Louis police board, quit. Governor Phil M. Donnelly named Priest as the new president. He accepted quickly.

Sam Priest served as head of the governor's board for two years and four months, until its tenure expired on February 1, 1949. He found the department still clinging to the past, although the atomic age had begun and so had the postwar crime surge.

Priest and his fellow board members foresaw that the nation and its great cities were at the beginning of a staggering crime wave that would grow tremendously and reach far into the future. With foresight, they made a start in getting St. Louis ready to meet the onslaught. Priest and the board laid the groundwork for future improvement.

In May 1946 Priest married Margaret Boeteler McDonald, daughter of John Dillon McDonald and granddaughter of Judge Jesse McDonald. She had attended Sarah Lawrence College in New York. A previous marriage to the former Francine Notrebe Bull in 1935 resulted in divorce.

Priest had been out of public life for eight years when James T. Blair became governor in 1957. One of Blair's first official acts was to appoint a blue ribbon board of St. Louis police commissioners. H. Sam Priest was named president. The other members were Russell L. Dearmont, a former president of the Missouri Pacific Railroad; Kenneth Teasdale, former president of both the Missouri and the St. Louis Bar Associations; and Alphonse G. Eberle, former dean of the Saint Louis University Law School.

After serving four years under Governor Blair, the accomplishments of the Priest police board were so impressive that in 1961 incoming Governor John M. Dalton reappointed the entire board, with Priest continuing as president. This was a recognition unequaled in the history of the board.

Also in 1961 Priest was asked to take over the presidency of the Automobile Club of Missouri. Ten courageous years of building a police force that is one of the best in the nation ended for Priest as he began a new career.

H. Sam Priest died on May 4, 1987.

James P. Hickok

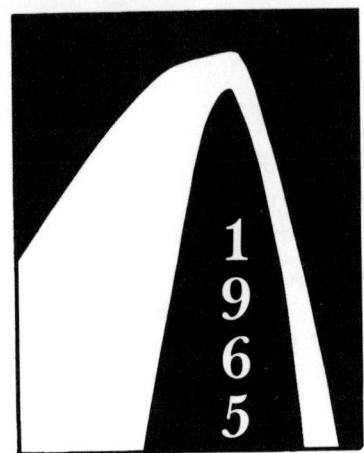

JAMES P. HICKOK STOOD in the great unfinished colosseum, as he had many times before, and the sight still filled him with wonder. In the crisp morning sunlight of the December day he saw high concrete walls ascending against the sky. He felt as though he was surrounded by cliffs as he looked far upward from the inside of the towering structure, which was a half-mile in circumference, covered a dozen acres, and had two massive decks that would seat 50,100 shouting people.

This tremendous circular sports stadium that was nearing completion in downtown St. Louis was something more than a brilliant architectural concept. And it was something more than a spacious and useful arena. Here a city that had drifted into dereliction was being saved. Here a new spirit of St. Louis was being born.

Wearing the hard hat of the workers around him, Hickok stood inside the huge stadium and watched with satisfaction the bulldozers pushing mounds of earth and the cranes swinging buckets of concrete into position for pouring.

Others had contributed a great deal, but no one was more responsible for making the downtown stadium a reality than James P. Hickok, chairman of the board and chief executive officer of the First National Bank in St. Louis. From its beginning, he had been the president of the Civic Center Redevelopment Corporation, the organization created to use private capital to build the stadium and other structures that turned a blighted region just south of the downtown district into a new thirty-one-block civic center. He was the chief of three incorporators of this organization and before that, headed the chamber of commerce survey committee that studied the feasibility of the stadium civic-center project and recommended that it be undertaken.

As a result of this undertaking with private funds, the sick area of aged buildings, mongrel parking lots, dirty streets, and fleabag hotels was wiped out and no longer threatened to infect the heart of metropolitan St. Louis with decay.

Through the years, no worthy fund-raising campaign was too small and no endeavor in behalf of the public welfare or civic progress was too large when Jim Hickok was needed. During 1965 he was president of the United Fund. Tirelessly he attended meetings, made talks, helped organize the campaign, made personal solicitations for funds, and stayed by the elbow of the chairman.

With an abiding interest in youth, Hickok began working zealously for the YMCA. He became a member of its metropolitan board of directors in 1942 and, during his three-year presidency of the board, 1952-55, spearheaded a successful expansion fund drive. When the YWCA needed money, he headed the campaign and served on its board of trustees as well.

Under Hickok's leadership, the First National Bank buildings were remodeled so they would be more attractive and friendly to the people using them. From there Hickok moved on to remodeling whole communities. This adventure in civic betterment was a warmup for the great stadium civic-center project many years later. The new stadium was essential to the St. Louis Cardinals baseball team and the St. Louis Cardinals football team.

Hickok was honored for his part in this intrepid adventure in downtown rehabilitation. In 1964 he received the St. Louis Award jointly with Preston Estep, vice-president of Civic Center Redevelopment Corporation and chairman of its executive committee. He was initiated into membership in the Academy of Squires, a group founded by Governor James T. Blair to honor Missourians for accomplishment and service at community, state, and national levels. He received this membership because of his devotion to civic welfare, his service to Westminster College, and his distinction as a banker.

Hickok was a member of the American Bankers Association, the Association of Reserve City Bankers, and the St. Louis Clearing House Association, of which he was president in 1958-59. He also served as president of the Missouri Bankers Association. He was a member of the National Conference of Christians and Jews, the National Museum of Transport, and the Backstoppers.

His various business affiliations included directorships in the St. Louis Union Trust Company, the Transit Casualty Company, the St. Louis National League Baseball Club, the Investment Securities Corporation, and the American Central Insurance Company.

Nearly forty of Hickok's years were spent as a banker, though it was a business he entered by chance, with no intention of staying with it permanently. He came to the First National Bank in 1950 as executive vice president, after heading several neighborhood banks. He was told he had graduated from the bush league to the big league when he moved downtown. He showed big league caliber and in 1957 was made president of the bank. In 1962 he became chairman of the board and chief executive officer.

His wife, the former Florence Brooks, who was once a Veiled Prophet maid of honor, said he came into the house with a briefcase full of work almost every night. Much of the work that filled the days and often the nights of Jim Hickok was not for the bank, but for the community. Much was done on his own time. The Hickoks had a son, James P. Hickok, Jr., and a daughter, Florence Brooks Kramer.

Jim Hickok attacked recreation with the same vigor, purpose, and determination that he did work. He went to the arctic circle in Canada to fish and down to the Caribbean Sea. He was completely absorbed in his collection of 75,000 stamps. He loved bridge and golf, although on the links he shot in the agonizing nineties. Nevertheless, the Bogey Club made him its president. His interest in football and baseball was always intense, and his association with the new sports stadium increased it. Politically, he was a Republican. He was an elder of Central Presbyterian Church.

"There are few people who don't like him and that, coupled with a good mind, may be other reason for his success," said one who worked closely with him. "It seems that he puts into it what is necessary to do the job—and then he puts in that little extra something, that extra inch, that extra mile."

James Parker Hickok was born on September 28, 1902, in Farmington, Missouri, then a country town of about 2,500 about seventy miles south of St. Louis. His father was the Reverend Chauncey Hickok, who was the preacher at Farmington's First Presbyterian Church, and his mother was Margaret Parker Hickok.

His forebears were early American stock, who came to Missouri from Virginia, but the only time the boy's interest in genealogy perked up was when he learned that the dauntless frontier lawman, "Wild Bill" Hickok, was a kinsman.

"He was the only one of the whole family I know of who ever amounted to much," he said.

After Hickok graduated from high school, he was off to Westminster

College, his father's alma mater, to prepare for the pulpit. "I majored in Greek, minored in philosophy, and went into banking. Now put that together," he said.

At the end of his sophomore year Hickok left the Westminster campus and was never to return as a student. But in later years he became a trustee, president of the board, and recipient of an honorary doctor of laws degree from the college.

Hickok resumed his studies at the University of Missouri at Columbia, partly because he could get a steady job there in the print shop and pay his way. In 1926 he received his bachelor of arts degree and decided to go on for a master's. He had been recommended for an assistant professorship at Columbia University in New York. At that point he had changed his goals and wanted to study international law and join the foreign diplomatic service, rather than go into the ministry.

Suddenly all his plans were knocked awry by the death of his father. He was offered a job and took it, as a seventy-five-dollar-a-month bookkeeper for the Arkansas National Bank at Hot Springs. He didn't think banking was for him, but the job would do until he found another. He disliked mathematics and had flunked trigonometry one semester at Westminster. It wasn't long before he found himself enjoying the work. That, he decided, was his career. In a couple of years he thought he would like to be a bank examiner and got a job as one, working in the Eighth Federal Reserve District out of St. Louis and Hot Springs.

Came the depression with its woes for banks and bankers, and in 1930 young Jim Hickok took over as cashier of the Clayton National Bank, which was in difficulty. In 1933 new management was installed at the Manchester Bank of St. Louis, and Hickok, who was showing increasing ability, was made executive vice-president. In 1935 he became president and did his first bank remodeling job.

In 1943 Hickok accepted the presidency of the Manufacturers Bank and Trust Company. By now Jim Hickok was getting a sizable reputation as a progressive, public-spirited banker who also had a zeal for serving the public welfare. He loved St. Louis and he loved people.

One of the enterprises watching him bring a new spirit to South Broadway was the First National Bank. It offered him a job as its executive vice-president. In 1950 the First National had made a momentous decision. There was then a gloomy and pervasive belief that downtown St. Louis was doomed by the blight and deterioration that was crawling toward it, by the growing traffic congestion, and by the tendency toward decentralization. The venerable and prestigious First National did not believe downtown was doomed. It decided to stand its ground and sink its foundations even deeper by modernizing and expanding. Jim Hickok's belief in the future of St. Louis and its downtown district was strengthened by this confidence. Ten years later he had a chance to show his own courage and faith in the area.

In 1958 Charles L. Farris, executive director of the city's Land Clearance for Development Authority, had a daring idea: Wipe out the blighted area south of downtown St. Louis by building a much needed sports stadium. It was the ideal spot, the most accessible in the metropolitan area. The Chamber of Commerce of Metropolitan St. Louis listened and thought the idea was good. It appointed a survey committee to study it and report on its feasibility. James P. Hickok was selected chairman.

The Hickok committee quickly decided that the downtown sports stadium and civic center idea had "tremendous potential." It followed up with engineering and economic studies, made by Sverdrup & Parcel. After studying the report of the engineering firm months later, the committee recommended the project, with Hickok stating that it was "economically feasible if St. Louisans will do their part."

It was essential to start the project with a big investment to get the ball rolling, and this came when Anheuser-Busch put up $5 million in one chunk. On the heels of this donation came more good news—the Cardinals would transfer their games from the old stadium on North Grand to the new one when it was completed. If St. Louis would build a stadium, there would be someone to use it.

After two months of hard work, $17.5 million of the equity capital was raised. Jim Hickok worked tirelessly on it, but he gave equal credit to Preston Estep.

St. Louis no longer lived on memories of the golden age of the steamboat, the World's Fair, and its status as the fourth city in America. The Gateway Arch, the Jefferson National Expansion Memorial, the Mill Creek Valley redevelopment, the Poplar Street free bridge, the new downtown sports stadium and civic center transformed it into a community of the future.

This transformation that changed St. Louis from a city of yesterday to a city of tomorrow was wrought by a new leadership that dared to do great things. It was a leadership that had faith in the people of St. Louis and gained their confidence as well. In the forefront of this leadership was James P. Hickok.

James P. Hickok died on April 30, 1977.

Charles Allen Thomas

1966

THE OLD AMUSEMENT PARK that had delighted generations of St. Louisans was gone. The gallant horses that circled rhythmically to the jaunty music of the carousel were no more. The mountainous roller coaster with its rumbling wheels and screams of thrill-seekers belonged to the past, and so did the fun house and the shooting gallery and the picnickers with their baskets. The last vestiges of an outdated era had been obliterated by bulldozers, cranes, and construction gangs.

Charles Allen Thomas, whose long career embodied that rare combination of brilliant scientist and distinguished business executive, stood on the site of what had been Forest Park Highlands and watched an elongated five-story building of red brick take shape on almost the exact spot where the roller coaster had undulated against the sky. The modern, functional structure was well on its way to completion and when finished would contain classrooms, laboratories, and administration offices. There would be a large library, too, and the old thirty-three-acre amusement park would have become Forest Park Community College. The new college would take care of first- and second-year students when it opened. It was one of three campuses of the St. Louis-St. Louis County Junior College District, where permanent buildings were erected with $47.2 million, which the people of the city and county voted at a remarkable bond issue election, an election which professional politicians were convinced couldn't be won.

With his overcoat buttoned against the raw wintry day, Monsanto's Charlie Thomas was not stepping his way over freshly graded clay on a mere sightseeing tour. He had a personal interest in the building. It was he who had led the amazing and unconventional campaign that persuaded the taxpayers of the city and county to give their money to bring

higher education to more future citizens.

A man with a public conscience, Charlie Thomas gave his time and energy generously to any task requested by his government or his community. But one of the biggest public welfare tasks of his lifetime he imposed upon himself—to work for more and better education of American youth, because the world was becoming intricately complex, and knowledge, judgment, and reason were needed to avoid disaster and to reach a higher level of civilization.

Charles Allen Thomas was one of the nation's top scientists who had a vital role in the development of the atomic bomb during World War II. And when the job was done, he was among that awed group of scientists who saw the first test of the A-bomb on the New Mexico desert. That blinding, world-changing flash, which released a power that could be used for immeasurable good or evil, burnt into his consciousness a statement of British novelist-historian H.G. Wells: "More and more the history of mankind is a race between education and catastrophe."

So when he was asked to head the bond drive for the community college, he consented and, laying aside all else, fought with evangelistic fervor, inspiring an enthusiastic band of amateur campaigners—students, faculty, and friends—to an unexpected victory.

Thomas' abiding interest in youth and education made him a frequent and inspiring speaker at graduation exercises all over the nation. For many years he served as curator of Transylvania College, with which he had close ties, and as a corporation life member of the Massachusetts Institute of Technology. He gave valuable service to Washington University and was elected chairman of its board of trustees. He was responsible for persuading Dr. James R. Killian, Jr., corporation chairman of MIT, to serve on the Washington University board.

Thomas' interest in building future Americans began in his boyhood. He had long been active on behalf of the American Boy Scouts and was a member of the advisory board of the St. Louis council. He ran his own Keewaydin Camp for boys in the rugged Canadian country 300 miles north of Toronto. And he was elected to the board of directors of the Herbert Hoover Boys Club of St. Louis.

His busy life as an industrial scientist and executive of the third largest chemical company in the United States did not keep him from giving time and energy to help welfare projects. Year after year he collected money for the United Fund, and in 1963 was elected president of the fund.

Born shortly after the dawn of 1900, Thomas was a vital member of that enterprising and imaginative band of scientists, technologists, engineers, inventors, builders, and thinkers who made the twentieth century the most fantastically progressive in the history of mankind, a century which advanced from the horse-and-buggy age to the space age. His work in the laboratory and in the thick-carpeted executive office contributed substantially to the chemistry revolution which changed living as much as did the industrial revolution of the last century.

During World War II, the government in Washington, D.C., called on Thomas for many services as scientist, coordinator, administrator, and adviser. The most fateful event of the twentieth century was the discovery of the key that unlocked the atom and released nuclear energy. Thomas was one of the scientists of the hush-hush Manhattan Project who had a major role in the development of the bomb.

After the war he was in the forefront of those who strove to turn the frightful nuclear sword into the most beneficial plowshare the world had known. He was one of a board of five consultants appointed by the state department to mull over the problem of the atom bomb and come up with an answer. After two months of almost constant discussion, they agreed on a plan for international control of the production of atomic energy, which was received with favor.

Honors came to Charles Allen Thomas from all directions. The American Chemical Society made him its president and chairman of its board. He was given the Perkin medal, the highest award for achievement in industrial chemistry, by the Society of Chemical Industries. He received the Priestley medal, the highest honor bestowed by the American Chemical Society; he was given the Gold Medal of the American Institute of Chemists and the Palladium Medal of the Societe de Chimie Industrielle. He was elected to membership in the National Academy of Science in 1948.

When he received the Medal for Merit, the highest civilian award bestowed by the United States, for his work in helping develop the atomic bomb, the citation read that he had "completed vital research and solved production problems . . . without which the bomb would never have been." He received the Industry Research medal, the Deeds-Kettering memorial award, the Missouri award for distinguished service in engineering, the Golden Plate award of the American Academy of Achievement, and others.

He was showered with honorary degrees by universities and colleges, among them were Washington, Saint Louis, Princeton, Brown, Alabama, Ohio Wesleyan, Lehigh, and Missouri universities. Hobart, Kenyon, and Transylvania colleges honored him. His business affiliations included membership on the boards of the First National Bank in St. Louis, the Metropolitan Life Insurance Company, Rand Corporation, St. Louis Union Trust, and Southwestern Bell Telephone. He worked for the revitalization of St. Louis through the Civic Center Redevelopment Corporation, of which he was a board member. He was a founder and board member of the St. Louis Research Council. He was also a founding member of the National Academy of Engineering.

At ten years of age, Charlie Thomas was already dabbling in chemistry. At seventeen he was a lieutenant in the army; at twenty he was a college graduate. He added almost four more years of graduate study to his formal education and at twenty-three had his first research job and was working on knocking the knock out of automobile engines.

At twenty-six Thomas opened his own laboratory in partnership with a close friend, Carroll A. (Ted) Hochwalt, and it grew rapidly, in spite of the fact that it exploded once and was slowed down by the depression. After ten years, Monsanto, which had been a customer, bought the laboratory. He and Hochwalt went to work for Monsanto.

Thomas used to say that he would never leave the laboratory to become an executive, but he did. He became a member of Monsanto's board of directors, just as that company was becoming a major part of the chemistry revolution which affected the daily life of so many Americans. At fifty-one, he succeeded to the presidency.

The years passed; they were good years. For nine of them he was president of Monsanto and for the next five, chairman of the board, succeeding Edgar M. Queeny, son of the founder.

For a change of pace and scenery, and for the fun of outdoor living, Charles and his wife, Margaret (most people called her Marnie) went to their 165-acre farm and hunting lodge in St. Charles County, where there were a half-dozen duck blinds and a skeet shooting range, plus hunting dogs, guns, and a comfortable rambling farmhouse. Or they went to their 12,000-acre magnolia plantation near Albany, Georgia, where they grew peanuts, corn, and soybeans and hunted quail.

"My real avocation is farming," Thomas said. It was an interest that stemmed from childhood, when he spent his early years on a Kentucky farm. He used his farmlands, too, for experimentation in the continuing search for better agricultural products.

Like most other executives, Thomas made many business trips and usually flew—either on commercial airlines or on one of Monsanto's own craft. In the 1930s he learned to fly himself and acquired a single-engine Waco of that period.

Charles Allen Thomas was born February 15, 1900, on a farm fourteen miles from Lexington in Kentucky's bluegrass country. His father, of Welsh descent, was a Disciples of Christ minister who died when Charlie was only six months old. His mother, Frances Carrick Thomas, was of Scotch-Irish descent and lived to be ninety-four years old.

"My mother was a great woman," Charlie Thomas said. "They named a library after her at Transylvania College. President Eisenhower came there for the dedication and I introduced him. He made a talk."

Two others made a big influence on Thomas' life—his aunt and his grandmother. Because no school was convenient, the women tutored Charlie as a child. When he finally went to school a few years later, he was far in advance of his age group.

The family moved to Lexington, directly across the street from Transylvania College, the oldest college west of the Alleghenies. When Charlie graduated from high school, he simply walked across the street. World War I came along, and young Charlie enlisted in the Student Army Training Corps and at seventeen was a lieutenant. He was packed off to Camp Perry, where he served as rifle instructor until the war ended. Out of this experience grew his love of hunting and shooting, which his wife shared.

Thomas received good science instruction at Transylvania. After graduating in 1920 he was sent by his mother and aunt to Massachusetts Institute of Technology for graduate study. There he met Henry (Hank) B. du Pont of the notable chemical du Ponts.

"He began to show an impatience with old ways and conventional approaches," Hank du Pont said twenty-three years later, when Thomas was given the Perkin medal. "He began to look beyond the obvious and seek out the unknown. In doing so, Charlie Thomas took his place beside other men in other fields who also were expressing discontent with easy answers and smug assurances. America was built by people who were eternally dissatisfied, eternally looking for something better. . . . Charlie Thomas is the most dissatisfied man I have ever known."

On finishing at MIT, Charlie and Hank headed for Dayton, Ohio, where jobs were available with the General Motors research laboratory. In 1923 Thomas was working on a team which was trying to cure the knocking engine. Also working in the laboratory was Ted Hochwalt, with whom he later formed the Thomas & Hochwalt Laboratories.

Hochwalt listed Thomas' successful attributes as imagination, curiosity, intuitiveness, buoyant enthusiasm, driving ambition, friendliness, an apparent unlimited supply of energy, and an amazing clairvoyance about future chemistry needs.

The first customer of the new firm was General Motors, which wanted a synthetic automobile tire. The laboratory, which started in the attic of a three-story building in downtown Dayton, flourished. The chemistry revolution was gaining momentum. At the end of ten years, Thomas & Hochwalt had moved out of the attic, built new facilities on seven acres at the edge of town, and increased its employees from one to 125. After Monsanto bought the laboratory, it became the central research department there.

As an assiduous scientist and industrialist, Charles Allen Thomas added to the standard of living and to the strength and vigor of the nation. And he found time to come out of the busy laboratory to make innumerable contributions to the betterment of his community and the welfare of its people.

Charles Allen Thomas died on May 2, 1977.

Charles Powell Whitehead

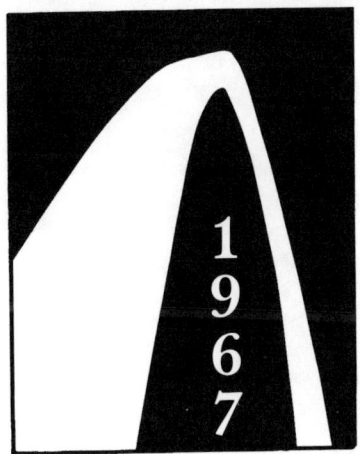

ON HIS TWENTIETH BIRTHDAY Charles Powell Whitehead began his career in the steel castings industry at a drawing board in the engineering department of the old Commonwealth Steel Company in Granite City, Illinois. But as a draftsman he had a formidable shortcoming. He couldn't draw.

That was fortunate. If he had been an adequate performer with a pencil, T-square, and slide rule, he might have spent the rest of his life bent over a drawing board. That would have been unfortunate—for his company, for the steel castings industry, and for the greater St. Louis community. Lost would have been one of this area's eminent business chieftains and a civic leader whose selfless public service to people on both banks of the Mississippi River will long be remembered.

Young Whitehead graduated from Culver Military Academy and soon after was commissioned to serve in the naval aviation forces during World War I. Looking around for a suitable career after his service, he turned to Commonwealth Steel Company and drafting. But after six months at the drawing board, Whitehead was moved to the company's shop, where there was less artistry, but more action and a better opportunity to observe the gritty fundamentals of the steel castings industry.

In a couple of years he was on the road as a salesman and roamed the West talking railroads into buying his company's cast steel products. He had a prodigious talent for selling, and it took him to the top. He moved up through the sales department to general management. He was eventually made president of the company, which by then had changed its name to General Steel Castings Corporation. Later it became known as General Steel Industries, Inc.

Charles Powell Whitehead was a warm, sympathetic man who dealt

directly with people during the tough years when he was on the road, getting to know them well. In his thorough and effective selling methods he talked to the foreman in the roundhouse, the overalled worker in the car shop, and the railroad executive in his plush office.

He didn't change when he became president of General Steel in 1945. He walked into his new office with an abiding conviction that industry, often as cold as the steel his company sold, should have a human side. He believed it had a responsibility and an obligation to give leadership in making the community in which it was located a better place to work, live, and enjoy life.

One memorable evening at the close of his many years leading General Steel, grateful East Side citizens gathered for a recognition dinner for Powell Whitehead. They bestowed awards and certificates on him and gave him a silver bowl. In the course of the evening fourteen speakers representing various facets of the community extolled him for his influence on the well-being of the community.

They told of his leading role in a successful campaign that raised $800,000—though the goal was only $650,000—to help build a six-story addition to the Granite City's St. Elizabeth's Hospital. The spectacular success of that drive was cited in Granite City's winning the 1958 All America City award from the National Municipal League and *Look* Magazine. They told of his part in a successful campaign to raise $120,000 for a Boy Scout camp, and of his tireless efforts to raise money for the United Fund and other similar causes. His energy, skill, imagination, and attitude made the Quad Cities economically stronger and gave them a more vibrant community spirit. And they stressed, too, the importance of his guidance and revitalization of General Steel, which gave employment to about 2,000 people in the community.

"I was only doing my job, and part of that is community work," responded the overwhelmed honoree. "I wanted to be a good citizen and wanted the company to be a good citizen."

Through the years Whitehead's impact went far beyond the neighborhood of General Steel. It was felt especially in the St. Louis community, where he lived and served the public welfare, applying the ability and experience he had gained in business.

Among the beneficiaries of his money-raising efforts were the Arts and Education and Saint Louis Symphony funds. In the early 1960s he was one of three recipients of the Brotherhood citation of the National Conference of Christians and Jews.

Whitehead became enthusiastic over constructing a library-herbarium and educational buildings at the Missouri Botanical Garden, which he believed was one of the community's finest assets. With a Noah-like urgency he also supported a rapid transit system for the St. Louis area "before it's too late."

After retiring from the presidency of General Steel Industries, Inc., in 1964, Whitehead maintained a St. Louis office for several years and served as a director and chairman of the finance company for the company.

Whitehead and his wife, Georgia (Zeibig), enjoyed family get-togethers with daughter Frances Remington, her husband, Tom, and their children. A favorite family retreat spot for his family was Harbor Point, Michigan. The Whitehead's son, Charles Powell, Jr., died during World War II of polio while serving as gunnery officer on a naval ship.

Both Powell and Georgia Whitehead found much pleasure in travel and through the years covered most of the globe. Many journeys were business trips for General Steel, since the company had overseas licenses and sold steel abroad. The Whiteheads traveled to Europe several times, to South Africa, the Far East, and most of South America. They visited West Berlin and spent several days in Moscow.

Charles Powell Whitehead once said that "however important or interesting the facts of yesterday may be, they can never engage our attention in the same way as the things we are doing today and the things we are planning for tomorrow."

Charles Powell Whitehead died on June 22, 1981.

Frederic M. Peirce

S T. LOUIS' DOWNTOWN UNDERWENT a remarkable renaissance between 1959 and 1968. A festering riverfront that was the doorway to the city and a region of rot just south of the business district were transformed by an inspired and determined civic leadership.

The Mississippi River no longer slipped by the cobbled levee as ashamedly as it once did, and flophouses no longer flourished at the southern fringe of the business district. There were modern office buildings, apartment houses, motels, garages, and even a revolving restaurant atop a hotel. New expressways sped automobiles to and from downtown. A stately new free bridge crossed the river at Poplar Street. A handsome new sports stadium brought cheering fans downtown.

In 1958, when this architectural transfiguration was beginning, but most of it was still in the dream stage, a stranger came to St. Louis from Hartford, Connecticut. He was Frederic M. Peirce, a widely esteemed insurance executive. He had just accepted the presidency of General American Life Insurance Company, which had its home office in a twelve-story building near downtown St. Louis.

Though he was well acquainted with those in the insurance field, few outside it recognized him when he walked along the streets of the city. He was not a stranger long, however; he was a man who made friends quickly.

Peirce's extraordinary abilities both as a businessman and as a civic leader were soon discovered. Leading St. Louisans who were trying to bring the laggard city abreast of the other great metropolitan areas called on him to lend a shoulder. General American had a tradition of involvement in community affairs.

Peirce had been in town only three years when he was made chair-

man of a citizens committee to raise a hard-to-get $2.6 million to complete equity financing of the proposed downtown sports stadium. His committee fulfilled its mission, and the stadium was assured. He became one of the many who contributed substantially to the new downtown skyline, but his interest in community betterment ranged far beyond creations in stone, steel, concrete, chromium, and glass.

Not many blocks behind the ethereal Gateway Arch began the ghettos and the blighted inner city. Here were ugly sores of human deprivation, of unemployment and frustration. The thoughts of pragmatic Fred Peirce and other businessmen turned to finding the means of helping disadvantaged people out of despondency, of making them useful, gainfully employed citizens.

Peirce believed that the role of business should be larger in trying to solve these important urban problems and that business should work jointly toward their solution with local government and other forces of the community. Soon he was one of the city's most effective civic leaders, chosen as chairman of Civic Progress. He and his colleagues began to examine racial problems in St. Louis and particularly unemployment. They held down-to-earth discussions with a cross-section of black leaders and tried to get a better understanding of their problems and needs.

It was about this time that the National Alliance of Businessmen was created in Washington with the purpose of finding work for the unemployed throughout the nation. The initial task was to put a total of 100,000 from the inner cities into the work force. The quota for the St. Louis district was 2,000.

Since the idea was along their line of thinking, Peirce and Civic Progress dropped their own plans and threw their weight behind the NAB drive. Peirce conducted the campaign from his office. There were days and nights full of work. A special effort was made to convince blacks of the sincerity of the undertaking.

The campaign was immensely successful. Instead of 2,000 jobs, the St. Louis drive got pledges of 3,122 jobs. In addition, some 6,000 summer jobs were found for needy youths from the inner city. Industry and business made a surprising discovery. As Peirce pointed out, "They found they had acquired some good employees." The St. Louis operation was copied all over the nation in other NAB campaigns.

Peirce was also in the forefront of an endeavor to improve the inadequate mass transportation system that had bogged down inexpensive travel in St. Louis and its environs, clogged the highways with automobiles, and immobilized those who did not own or drive a car.

He was a willing fund-raiser for the sick, the needy, the aged, and the otherwise unfortunate. He was a stalwart of the United Fund, serving in all capacities. A businessman who had a sensitive social conscience, Peirce believed that what increased the welfare of one segment of the community increased the welfare of all.

Peirce's friends looked upon him as a man of complete integrity. He was pithily described as a "down-to-earther." His dynamic leadership of the NAB jobs campaign and its consequent contribution to black-and-white amity caught the popular imagination and led directly to his selection as the recipient of the St. Louis Award.

Among the greatest achievements in his life was his appointment as a director of the Federal Reserve Bank of St. Louis and his designation as chairman of the board. Early in 1966 he was named to the Washington University board of trustees; he was also a member of the president's council of Saint Louis University.

In 1968 Peirce was appointed a member of the board of trustees of the Danforth Foundation, which formerly had confined its board members to professional educators. He received a citation from the National Conference of Christians and Jews for his work in improving race relations.

The breadth of Peirce's impact on the community was indicated by a record of his activities. He was a director of Anheuser-Busch, World Color Press, Alton Boxboard Company, and General Steel Industries. He was vice-president of the St. Louis Area Boy Scouts Council, a director of the chamber of commerce, and a member of the advisory board of the YWCA. He was a director of the Municipal Theatre Association, a trustee of the Law Enforcement Foundation, a trustee of the Missouri Public Expenditure Survey, a director of the Urban Redevelopment Corporation, the Urban League, and the St. Louis Research Council.

He was chairman of the Life Insurance Association of America, a director of the Institute of Life Insurance, a trustee of the American College of Life Underwriters, and a member of the Life Underwriters Association, as well as the St. Louis Life General Agents and Managers Association.

He was a director of the Metropolitan St. Louis Hospital Planning Commission, a member of the advisory council of KETC, and on the board of the Saint Louis Symphony Orchestra. He belonged to these clubs: Advertising, Ambassadors, Bellerive County, Bogey, Missouri Athletic, Noonday, Racquet, Round Table, St. Louis, and Stadium.

Frederick M. Peirce was born in Cambridge, Massachusetts, on January 23, 1910. He was the son of Edwin W. Peirce and Frances Quick

Peirce. At that time his father was a YMCA secretary in Boston. His grandfather had been a Methodist minister. The family name was originally Pers, but somehow became Peirce in the New World.

When young Fred was eight (he had three older sisters, including a pair of twins), the family moved to Fort Wayne, Indiana. His next move, at age fifteen, was to Omaha, Nebraska, where his father had been made general secretary for the Y.

He entered Omaha's North High School as a senior and a stranger, but soon made many friends. He was on the debating team and began thinking of becoming a lawyer. Midway through his senior year romance blossomed. He began paying attention to Virginia Jay, a classmate and a descendant of John Jay, the nation's first chief justice. They became high school sweethearts.

Virginia's father was transferred to Devils Lake, North Dakota, and when school was out, she joined her family there. The two corresponded regularly, but it was a lonesome summer for Fred. He got a job in a steel foundry at $19.80 a week and saved his money. Then he blew it all on a visit to Devils Lake.

That fall Fred went to Omaha University, a small school that became part of the University of Nebraska. He was still determined to become a lawyer. A popular student, he was class president in his second year and made Beta Theta Pi. Because there wasn't enough money available, he had to spend a year working for a wholesale paint company, rather than attending Northwestern University, his goal.

That was 1929. Shortly after the stock market crash, the wheels of industry slowed. The number of unemployed mounted. "I was a casualty of the depression," Peirce said. "I never got back to college and had to pass up the chance to become a lawyer."

The paint company closed its Omaha branch and transferred Peirce to its district office at Kansas City, where his salary was cut three times and where he saw the personnel shrink from thirty-two to six. Nonetheless, he became district manager.

In 1931 Virginia Jay returned to Omaha. She and Fred saw each other again and on Christmas Eve of that year they became engaged. But the young couple—Peirce was twenty-two—decided to postpone the wedding until the depression was over. After all, Washington claimed that prosperity was just around the corner.

But as dismal 1933 moved in and the depression deepened, they changed their minds. "We decided that the depression had become a way of life," said Peirce. "Virginia was making sixty dollars a month and I was making $110. We got married and rented an apartment in

Kansas City for $47.50 a month."

Peirce began selling paint, with a territory of all of Missouri except for St. Louis. After months of traveling, he decided that was not the way he wanted to live. "I was finally persuaded to leave the paint business and go into the insurance business," he said.

In the fall of 1937 he went to work for the John Hancock Mutual Life Insurance Company in Omaha. Between then and 1940 he was successively cashier, agent, and supervisor for the agency. Next he wanted experience in home office work and in 1940 joined the staff of Capitol Life in Denver.

Life was good in Denver for the Peirces. Their first child, Barbara, was born there in 1941. His son, John Frederic, was born there in 1947. Peirce got the experience he wanted in all phases of the insurance business.

In May 1947 Peirce joined the Life Insurance Agency Management Association, an umbrella organization which covered the United States and Canada. He started as a senior management consultant and rose quickly. From 1949 to 1953 he was associate director of the company relations division, then was assistant to the managing director. In 1956 he became director of institutional relations and the same year became managing director.

He enjoyed the work. He traveled about half the time, and Virginia was able to go with him. He was exposed to the best brains and highest capabilities in the insurance business.

"I expected to stay with the association the rest of my life," he said. "It was a nice life. We loved Hartford, the New England mountains, and the sea."

But something happened to change that life. In December 1957 two automobiles collided in a snowstorm in Washington, D.C. Killed instantly was Powell B. McHaney, St. Louis civic leader and president of General American Life Insurance Company.

The company needed a new president and offered the job to Peirce. He accepted. After ten years he was named chairman of the board of directors and chief executive officer. He had come from being a stranger in town to being a top civic leader.

"Frederic M. Peirce loved St. Louis," said an associate. "I think he wanted to make it the best city in America."

Frederic M. Peirce died on May 13, 1974.

James S. & William A. McDonnell

1969

THEY CAME HERE AS STRANGERS—these two brothers—but they became widely known and each in his own way did much to make the St. Louis community a better place.

One of the brothers was an aeronautical engineer with a pioneering mind, and his face was turned to the sky. He had worked with aircraft—and had flown them, too—since the days when they were made of wood, wire, and fabric.

The other was a lawyer who had turned banker because the world of finance fascinated him.

James S. McDonnell was the aeronautical brother. He came to St. Louis in 1939 full of ideas for designing and manufacturing aircraft which would go higher, faster, and farther than any yet made. With these dreams he scraped together enough money from friends, relatives, and his own savings to start a small aircraft company on the edge of Lambert Field. He had a one-room establishment and hopes that orders would come in before his capital ran out.

William A. McDonnell, the banker brother, came to St. Louis five years later, in 1944, to take the vice-presidency of a large bank. The position had been offered to him because of his achievements elsewhere and his growing reputation as a leader in the field of banking.

For the brothers McDonnell it was a reunion. They had last been together here when their mother brought them from Little Rock, Arkansas, to spend four weeks at the 1904 World's Fair, when Jim was five and Bill was going on ten.

James Smith McDonnell became familiarly known as "Mr. Mac," and his employees became his "teammates." The McDonnell Aircraft Corporation, the company he founded, headed, and helped to develop

James S. McDonnell

William A. McDonnell

became a mammoth enterprise and built some of the world's best fighter planes, with its masterpiece the incomparable twin-jet Phantom II, which was the stalwart of the skies above Vietnam.

The company contributed immeasurably to the defense of the United States and went on to pioneer in space exploration. From its own research and experimentation it built the historic Mercury and Gemini spacecraft, which took the first Americans into orbit and brought them back again safely. And the McDonnell spacecraft gave the United States the lead in the exploration of space and in the race to put the first man on the moon.

The sprawling aerospace company that Jim McDonnell built was also a boon to the economy of the St. Louis area; it became the largest employer in Missouri. It channeled a huge amount of its purchases to thousands of area subcontractors, adding to its beneficent impact on the economy. And the company that began on a shoestring merged with the huge Douglas Aircraft Company of Santa Monica, California, making the resultant McDonnell Douglas Corporation the second largest aerospace enterprise in the United States.

William Archie McDonnell, the elder of the two brothers, had achieved distinction as a banker and civic leader long before coming to St. Louis. Within a few years his ability, warmth, wit, and willingness to take on any chore which would promote the public welfare, made him a leader in the city. He soon became head of the large and prestigious First National Bank in St. Louis. From this influential pinnacle he put into everyday practice his philosophy that the banker has a responsibility to use his opportunities for civic betterment.

Just performing his banking duties gave Bill McDonnell a crowded calendar, but he found time to work with the Chamber of Commerce of Metropolitan St. Louis and for two years served as chairman of its board. Since its establishment, he was a member of and former president of Civic Progress. He was also interested in the welfare of youth and was active in Boy Scout affairs. He served as president of the St. Louis Area Council, Boy Scouts of America.

Bill McDonnell gained national recognition as a banker. He was a member of the executive committee of the American Bankers Association and served it in various other capacities. A high spot in his career was his election to the presidency of the Association of Reserve City Bankers, whose membership is limited to the senior executive officers of the nation's major banks. He was a director of the Federal Reserve Bank for six years and served for two years as a member of the Federal Advisory Council.

When Bill McDonnell came to St. Louis, the city had become a straggler in the forward march of the nation's large cities. He soon joined with a handful of imaginative and courageous civic leaders who retrieved the dream that had been lost and fired St. Louis with a new spirit—the spirit of renaissance.

Perhaps his finest moment in civic leadership came near the close of the 1940s when stagnation threatened downtown St. Louis. A good many businesses and some financial houses were wondering if the time had come for a westward exodus. Was downtown doomed?

The decision to run or stay squarely faced the First National Bank in St. Louis, because its building at Broadway and Locust was outdated and an expansion of its banking quarters was needed. The directors were divided on whether to build at a new location or stay with the old. It was a momentous decision, because other downtown businesses would be strongly influenced by what the venerable First National did.

Bill McDonnell, who was then president of the bank, recommended to the directors that the bank stay at its downtown location and they endorsed his decision.

In this and many other ways the McDonnell brothers contributed heavily to the progress of the St. Louis community. Especially they sought to advance the quality of education and the opportunities to acquire it.

Mr. Mac gave much of his time to serving on the board of trustees of Washington University and on the board of directors of Washington University Medical School and associated hospitals. In earlier years he served as chairman of both boards and at one time gave more than fifty hours a month to these educational activities.

When someone was needed to head a drive, the one likely to be called upon was Bill McDonnell, whose leadership, warmth, and speaking ability assured success. Only four years after he had arrived in St. Louis he was chosen to head the Community Chest campaign, the most important annual fund drive. It was so successful that in 1955 he was asked to lead the crucial first drive of its successor, the United Fund.

The McDonnell brothers were members of a prosperous, well-educated Arkansas family which liked to think of itself as Scots Presbyterian. James Smith McDonnell, Sr., their father, had come from Alabama, where he had graduated from the state university. Their mother, Susan Belle Hunter of Star City, Arkansas, was a graduate of Judson Institute. The McDonnells had three sons and a daughter.

William was born November 20, 1894, in Altheimer, Arkansas. It was on a railroad about thirty-five miles southeast of Little Rock. His father ran a general merchandise store there and did an extensive business with cotton farmers. When Bill was about four his mother went to Denver for her health, and James was born there. When mother and children came back from Denver, the family made its home permanently in Little Rock.

"I don't think I was ever given allowance," Bill said. "Our parents wanted to impress on us that we had to work for our money." A paper route of several miles had an important part in the upbringing of both boys.

"Jim was a good student," Bill reminisced. "His engineering propensities showed up early. He had the top of our house filled with wireless telegraphy apparatus. His interest in aviation came later."

Bill went away to Vanderbilt in 1912, took a liberal arts course for a couple of years, then switched to law for three more years. He graduated summa cum laude in 1917, receiving the university's Founders Medal for being the best in his class.

The United States had entered World War I; he enlisted in the army after he had passed the bar examination. He was commissioned as a first lieutenant in the heavy artillery and was promoted to captain in France, where he arrived at the front in time to participate in the last days of the war.

"By the time I returned from France, Jim was gone," said Bill, "and he never returned to Little Rock to stay."

Bill became general counsel for a Little Rock bank and became so fascinated with the world of finance that he abandoned law after eight years and went into the banking business with Little Rock's Federal Bank and Trust Company. He later became executive vice-president of the Commercial National Bank, where he remained until summoned to St. Louis.

In 1944 the old Mercantile-Commerce Bank and Trust Company offered him a position as vice-president, and he came to St. Louis. Jim had come to St. Louis five years earlier and the little aircraft company he had started on the edge of the airport had become a multi-million dollar enterprise by then. Bill became a director and acquired stock.

Soon the helpful, affable, and able Bill McDonnell had won many friends, and the towering First National Bank in St. Louis had taken him on as executive vice-president, with assurance that he would soon be promoted to the presidency. By 1957 Bill reached the mandatory retirement age and stepped down from nine years in the presidency to become chairman of the board.

In 1965 his wife, Carolyn, won distinction as a *Globe-Democrat* Woman of Achievement. The couple had two children: Sanford Noyes McDonnell, who later became chairman of McDonnell Douglas; and Cherry (Mrs. John L.) Swasey.

Just when young James S. McDonnell began reaching up toward the stars is uncertain, but it may have started when he got his first ride in an old barnstorming crate with a ninety-horsepower engine.

"It was the first time I went up in an airplane, and I liked it," he said. "It confirmed the interest I felt I had in aviation. I did my best to try to get into the Signal Corps Aviation Service in World War I. That later became the U.S. Air Force. However, I wound up serving seven months as a buck private in the regular army instead."

At Princeton for the next four years he wrapped his mind around physics and other studies and let nothing divert him. He graduated in 1921 with a bachelor of science degree and an awareness of what he wanted to do with his life. He wanted to be an aeronautical engineer.

"In those early days of flight, Massachusetts Institute of Technology was the only college in the western hemisphere that had a course leading to a master's degree in aeronautical engineering," he said, "so I entered it."

After M.I.T. he joined the Army Air Force Reserve and was off to Brooks Field at San Antonio to learn about flying in practice as well as theory. He planned to learn all he could about aircraft design and manufacture, and when he reached the age of forty, start his own business.

He moved around the country, getting experience and bettering himself along the way. He became a vice-president, engineer, and test pilot for various firms. He went to work for the Glenn L. Martin Company in Baltimore in 1933 and rose to chief project engineer. Near the end of 1938, as he was approaching his fortieth birthday, he made the decision to start his own business.

For various reasons, he decided that St. Louis was the right location for his venture. He rented a small office on the second floor of the old American Airlines building at Lambert Field. The advent of his company in mid-1939 was both inconspicuous and inauspicious.

Business was slow at first, but soon the European nations were slugging it out in World War II, and orders began to arrive. From then on the company's growth was spectacular.

The first big break came on New Year's Eve, 1942, when Mr. Mac got a telephone call from Washington. His company had won a contract to build the world's first carrier-based jet fighter. It was no accident. Typically, foresighted McDonnell had been long researching that new power, jet propulsion.

The plane built was the twin-jet Phantom I—McDonnell pioneered and has always led in the twin-jet field—and it was followed by the highly successful Banshee of Korean War fame. There were more fighters with spirit name—the Voodoo and Demon—and then came the famed Phantom II.

After years of building aircraft, Mr. Mac and his company soared into space. It was again the result of assiduous research which the company itself financed. It was far ahead of its competitors when in January 1959 NASA selected it to build Mercury, America's first manned orbital spacecraft. In April 1963 it was given the contract to create Gemini, the bigger and better two-man spacecraft. Its completely successful orbitings ended in November 1966. The McDonnell spacecraft had written a brilliant chapter in space history.

Those were great days for Mr. Mac. Frequently he had breakfast with the astronauts before their blast-off, watched their fiery launchings, and followed their flights from the blockhouse. Often his voice crackled over the public address system at his plant as he gave his employees messages or congratulations. "This is old Mac calling all the team. . . ."

While working for the Martin company in Baltimore in 1934, James S. McDonnell was married to Mary Elizabeth Finney, daughter of Dr. John T. M. Finney of Baltimore, an internationally known surgeon. She died in 1949 and the McDonnell family gift of $4.7 million to erect the new Washington University Medical Science Building is a memorial to her. They had two children, James Smith McDonnell III and John Finney McDonnell.

On Easter Sunday 1956, Jim McDonnell married Mrs. Priscilla Brush Forney of Greenwich, Connecticut. She had three children by a previous marriage.

Jim McDonnell became a staunch supporter of the United Nations. His company was the only one in the world that gave its employees a fully paid holiday each year on the anniversary of the founding of the UN. McDonnell was national chairman of a twentieth anniversary commemorative book published by the United Nations Association of the USA, and he served on its national board of directors. In an article written for that book, he linked the quest for peace with the vast potential of the space age. He wrote:

"I believe that space science and exploration are here to stay and will continue at a high rate of activity. The nature of man is such that man wants to discover and explore everything that he is able to discover and explore. Man's flight from the earth to the moon and planets will be the most prodigious adventure in his history to date. The hard work, the self-discipline and the soaring spirit of man which has brought him to the brink of this great achievement will not stop now. I believe it will have no end as long as man exists effectively on earth.

"The Space Age handwriting is on the wall: Man must recognize his responsibility for the constructive use of space. It may not be for those now living to achieve all the goals of the UN charter," he added, "but it is for those now living to give full measure of their time, their talents, and their wealth in striving toward these goals."

One of Bill McDonnell's favorite quotations came from Robert Louis Stevenson: "To travel hopefully is a better thing than to arrive and the true success is to labour." The McDonnell brothers traveled and labored effectively at a time in life when many men had left the road.

James S. McDonnell died on August 22, 1980. William A. McDonnell died on January 28, 1988.

Maurice R. Chambers

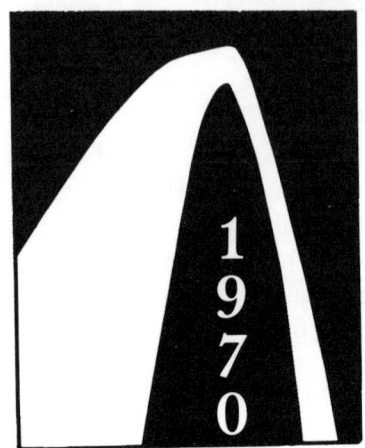

THERE WERE NEARLY TWENTY YEARS when St. Louis was only a memory to Maurice R. Chambers. He spent his boyhood here until he was fourteen. Then his family moved away. Here he acquired the nickname "Dude," which stuck to him, even though his sartorial tastes usually tended toward the conservative.

While in St. Louis he heard his father and grandfather, both traveling shoe salesmen, tell enthralling stories of the old days on the road—of the romance and excitement and hardships—and he may have been influenced to become a part of the shoe business begun by those men.

When Dude Chambers returned to St. Louis after nearly twenty years, it was as a towering figure in the shoe industry, an industry that had made the city famed throughout the world. By 1970 he was the head of Interco, Incorporated, a diversified giant of which the International Shoe Company was the greatest of nine components. As chairman of the board and chief executive officer of the huge organization, he was a force not only in the world of commerce, but in the community.

In 1949, when Chambers came back to St. Louis, he found that it was lagging behind many other great cities of America. The downtown district that had fascinated him as boy had evidently been standing still. It had not kept pace with the times. But through a new kind of vigorous leadership, St. Louis shook off its lassitude and moved abreast of urban progress elsewhere. Chambers was in the forefront of this dynamic leadership which created the new and soaring spirit of St. Louis.

He found at the International Shoe Company an organization that had a sense of public responsibility and a social conscience. When, after a spectacular business career he was made president in 1962, he took the opportunity to take a part in making St. Louis a better place in which

to live.

"I feel," he said, "that a fellow who has been as lucky as I have been in life should give some of it back."

His endeavors in behalf of civic betterment, education, health and hospitalization, help for the unfortunate, preservation of cultural values, and the general advancement of community welfare were remarkable.

There was no better measure of the stature of his civic leadership than the fact that he served two terms as president of Civic Progress. His eagerness to help the unfortunate of his community found early expression in his efforts for the United Fund. In 1962 the fund put him on its board of directors and sent him out to chair various fund-raising committees. In 1965 he was picked to lead the whole campaign.

His interest in youth, in preparing the young for their future roles as citizens and leaders, increased, rather than diminished as a result of the unrest and violence of the 1960s. He was worried deeply by campus turmoil—he was a trustee of Washington University—and the ugly menace of drugs, but he felt that "everything is going to come out all right if we work hard enough."

His work with youth found realization in such groups as the Boy Scouts, whom he felt had a great role ahead, the YMCA, and Junior Achievement ("they learn to run their own businesses under free enterprise"). He was on the boards of all three and was chairman of the Camporee in Forest Park in 1970, when 10,000 Scouts observed the sixtieth anniversary of their organization.

Although his formal education ended at the high school level, the world of higher education reached out to avail itself of his keen judgment, penetrating analysis, and overall business acumen. In addition to serving on Washington University's board, he was a member of the president's council of Saint Louis University.

A concern for the community's health and hospitals led him to give much of his time to Barnes Hospital and to serve on the board of trustees. In his striving to make St. Louis a better community, he was a stalwart of the chamber of commerce, serving on its board of directors and as an officer. He also served on the boards of the Missouri Public Expenditures Survey, the Convention Board of Greater St. Louis, the Governmental Research Institute, the Better Business Bureau, the Municipal Theater Association, the Arts and Education Council and the City Art Museum. In addition he was on the board of the Salvation Army and an ardent supporter of its activities. He and his wife attended St. John's Methodist Church.

Chambers was honored with the Mark A. Edison Award given by

members of the shoe industry who achieved outstanding records for civic service in their communities, and he was named by Governor Warren E. Hearnes to Missouri's Academy of Squires for his services to the state.

Many of his fellow businessmen saw Chambers as a forthright, unassuming fellow who was plainspoken and direct, who said what he meant and was unequivocal about where he stood. He made no effort to impress anyone. He knew his business, knew what he was talking about, and ran a taut, efficient company. He was very popular with his associates, but in business was a tough, no-nonsense guy.

Dude Chambers came to International Shoes from New York, where he had been the top shoe buyer for Montgomery Ward. He decided to return to St. Louis because he wanted to get into the manufacturing side of the shoe business. Instead, he was given the chore of selling shoes to large-volume chains.

In 1952 he was made general merchandise manager in the women's division and in 1956 became vice-president in charge of sales. A year later he was elected to the board of directors. In 1962 he reached the top when he was made president of the company and became one of the most admired business executives in town.

It was Chambers' idea to diversify. The upshot of his plan was a major reorganization which resulted in the creation of a new parent company called Interco, Incorporated, which covered nine major operating divisions and subsidiaries. Far-flung Interco was an umbrella over forty-six shoe factories, twenty-five apparel manufacturing plants, some 400 department stores, 800 retail shoe store and departments, and sundry service and supply facilities. Altogether, 35,000 people were employed by Interco in 1970.

Dude Chambers was one of the few top executives who lived in the city. His home was near Forest Park. He liked living there. "I have to be downtown a lot at night, so it's convenient," he said. "And I can't take this bumper-to-bumper driving to work any more." Chambers and his wife, Mildred ("Babe"), moved about thirty times after they were married as his career advanced. They have a married daughter, Cynthia Ruth Berg.

Whenever he had the time to play, Chambers played hard. "I'm a lousy golfer, but I love to play," he said. "I love to play gin rummy. [Friends say he was a formidable opponent at the card table.] I love football, baseball, and hockey. I like loafing on a small farm we have up in Pike County, but I don't raise anything much."

Maurice R. Chambers was born on July 14, 1916, on the hilltop area overlooking the west central city limits known as Hi-Pointe. His father was also named Maurice, and his mother was the former Ruth E. Brooks. One Easter day, young Chambers walked into the family gathering resplendent in a Little Lord Fauntleroy suit popular at the time. His grandfather couldn't suppress his admiration for this sartorial splendor. "He looks like a regular dude," he observed with enthusiasm. From then on, Maurice became Dude Chambers to all.

Dude was in high school when he was uprooted from St. Louis. His father got a job as a traveling salesman for the Tweedie Footwear Corporation in Jefferson City, and the family moved there. To earn his own spending money while in high school, Dude also got a job at the Tweedie company, working afternoons and nights.

"I got fifteen dollars a month," he recalled. "Every ten days I was paid five dollars."

When he was sixteen, Dude got a vacation job working with a Tweedie salesman. His earnings were meager, but his experience was invaluable, and he got a taste of the life of a traveling salesman. Next he worked nights at the soda fountain of the Crown Drug Company while attending school during the day.

"Some months after following this exhausting schedule, I decided to quit high school," said Chambers tersely. "So I just didn't go any more."

He continued working at the drugstore until he was offered a job at the dime store across the street for a dollar more a week. Then he learned that Tweedie had an opening for a salesman, and he was again in the shoe business—as he was to be for the rest of his life.

He was on the road most of the time; his territory consisted of eight or ten states in the Midwest. "They gave me a car which I could use at home," he remembered. "It gave style to my courting." He had begun pursuing Mildred Bartlett, who was in her last year at Jefferson City High School. Every weekend he rushed home to see her.

After two years of selling on the road, Tweedie gave Chambers the task of operating a failing shoe store in Waterloo, Iowa, and bringing it back into the black. Now his girlfriend would be 240 miles away.

On one trip to Jefferson City, Babe put an end to their frustration by stipulating that their marriage would take place on June 30, 1937. "She said the wedding would be held at her mother's home," Chambers said, "and she told me to be sure to be there."

After a year in Waterloo, the couple returned to Jefferson City. Again Dude was without a job, but he quickly found one managing the shoe department in Millsap's Department Store. Later he opened his own business, Chambers Shoe Store, which expanded to two other locations.

"We weren't rich, but we were making a little money," he recalled.

"Then the war began with all its problems. I had a chance, so I sold the three stores."

In 1941 he and Babe moved to Kansas City, where he went to work for Montgomery Ward as merchandiser for the company's shoe division, covering 130 stores. After a year, he was sent to New York for another two years as assistant buyer. Then he was reassigned to Kansas City for a period and promoted back to New York.

Occasionally he visited St. Louis to buy shoes. Old memories were stirred. He enjoyed New York City but decided he was a Midwesterner at heart. And what better place to live than in the shoe capital of the world?

"I came back to St. Louis with the intention of going to work for Brown Shoe Company," Chambers said. "But while I was waiting, I talked to Henry Rand, then head of International Shoe. He offered me a job and I took it."

His affection for St. Louis grew through the years. For him, downtown—its buildings, streets, people, and activity—again had the indefinable fascination for him it had when he was a boy.

Maurice R. Chambers died on October 14, 1990.

Howard F. Baer

1971

THERE WAS A BIT OF LOVE at first sight the day that Howard F. Baer got his first good look at St. Louis. The large buildings, the busy traffic, the milling shoppers fascinated him as he explored the downtown district. He liked the mood of the city that was about to become his new and permanent home.

He also liked the people he saw. He got the impression that they were warm and hospitable, friendly and substantial—a little different from the inhabitants of other large cities he had known.

The year 1927 was beginning when Howard Baer, together with his bride of six months, came to St. Louis to live. It was the year that a theater on Grand Boulevard showed the first talking movie, *The Jazz Singer*. It was also the year that an erstwhile airmail pilot named Charles A. Lindbergh drove the world wild with adulation by flying the *Spirit of St. Louis* nonstop from New York to Paris.

Howard Baer came to St. Louis to enter the business world. He joined the A. S. Aloe Company, a firm dating back to 1860 which dealt in surgical and optical equipment. Baer was twenty-five that year and not long graduated from Princeton. His love for St. Louis and its people grew and endured. His beneficent labors for the community were so arduous and time-consuming that he became a sort of full-time unpaid public executive after he retired from Aloe.

His greatest love was for the St. Louis Zoo. He was appointed to the Zoological Board of Control by Mayor Raymond Tucker in 1956 and was its president for ten years. He visited the zoo every day, devising ways of raising money for it. He persuaded Charles H. Yalem, financier and philanthropist, to donate $250,000 toward a children's zoo, an immensely popular feature. He was a prime mover in establishing the

miniature railroad. He was full of new ideas for the improving the zoo and in his travels visited dozens of zoos in America and Europe to learn more. The St. Louis Zoo changed in concept under his influence.

His next project was the airport. When he might have been fishing off the Bimini coast, playing endless rubbers of bridge, reading from his well-stocked library, or just basking in the sweet idleness of retirement, he was fighting a bruising battle. At the request of Mayor Alfonso J. Cervantes, he led a crucial campaign in St. Louis for voter passage of a $200 million revenue bond issue to improve and expand the airport facilities.

Under Baer's leadership, the 1968 bond issue won a walloping five-to-one victory at the polls. The following year Baer was given the St. Louis Award for his service to the city.

In 1971 he won a much harder victory at the polls. In an astonishing triumph which surprised even chronically optimistic Baer, the vote rescued the zoo, the City Art Museum, and St. Louis County's struggling Museum of Science and Natural History. The election also brought about the miracle of city and county residents agreeing on a mutually beneficial project—creating a city-county taxing district which was to provide ample funds to keep the three institutions thriving in the future.

When Washington University gave Baer an honorary bachelor of laws degree for being an exemplar of ideal community service in 1971, the speaker declared that because of Baer's successful campaign to win adequate tax support for the three institutions, "generations of St. Louisans who love art and nature will be for decades in his debt."

Two years after Howard Baer arrived in St. Louis from Charleston, West Virginia, he became president of A. S. Aloe Company. As the firm prospered and increased in size under his guidance, he went on to become one of the city's outstanding business leaders. But he was not content solely with the satisfactions of material success. Very early he encountered outstanding civic leaders, such as David R. Calhoun, Jr., and Benjamin Loeb, and they showed him how to live a fuller life through service to others.

Baer began by joining the Big Brothers Organization. His first sizable humanitarian chore was to head a Jewish Federation drive. He helped out in the community's annual charity campaigns, conducted through the years by United Charities, Community Chest, and United Fund. He served them all. He reached the top in this field in 1948, when he was chairman of the Community Chest drive. He did his job well. Demands for his services in civic and humanitarian causes multiplied.

A major factor in Baer's life was the National Conference of Christians and Jews, which sought brotherhood among various racial and religious groups. He served as Jewish co-chairman of the St. Louis area and was the St. Louis chairman of Brotherhood Week.

He also was a devoted member of the board of the Municipal Opera Association, which gave him a chance to indulge his lifelong enthusiasm for the theater. And he was on the board of the Saint Louis Symphony Society. He was a trustee of the Missouri Blue Cross Plan from 1936 to 1964 and served a three-year term as chairman of the board.

Baer received many honors, including the Legion of Merit from the army, an honorary degree from Washington University, and the American Institute of Aeronautics and Astronautics Civic Award.

In the business world he held directorships on the boards of the First National Bank, the St. Louis Union Trust Company, and the Angelica Company. He belonged to the Noonday Club, St. Charles Club, St. Louis Club, Princeton Club of New York, the Round Table, Westwood Country Club, and the University Club.

Howard F. Baer was born on June 10, 1902, in Charleston, the capital of West Virginia. It was then a pretty little town of about 20,000 on the Kanawha River. His father, David Baer, left Germany at the age of sixteen and reached the United States in 1882. Eventually he became a salesman for a wholesale liquor firm, though he was virtually a nondrinker. Howard's mother was the former Mayme Loewenstein, an energetic woman who was ambitious for her three children.

To pay for some major family illnesses and expensive schooling, his parents led a simple life with no frills. When Howard graduated from grade school, his mother decided he would attend no ordinary high school. Off he went to Choate, an excellent preparatory school at Wallingford, Connecticut.

By the time he graduated from Choate, his mother had Ivy League ideas. So Howard went to Princeton, which was not far from New York City and Broadway. Princeton was a happy choice. Young Howard was avidly interested in literature. He wanted to be a writer. Since his inclination tended toward the theater, his efforts centered largely on playwriting.

During his sophomore year a fellow student asked a Smith College girl to a prom. The girl had consented with the condition that he get a date for her twin sister. So Howard Baer went on a blind date and met Isabel Aloe. They saw each other from time to time. The relationship grew into a romance.

"By the end of my junior year," he said, "I was hooked. It was the Big Deal."

After graduation he might have gone to New York and pursued a career in the theater except for a very practical mother and uncle back in Charleston. The uncle was the president of the thriving Charleston National Bank.

Baer recalled, "On graduation the order came from home to cut out that stuff about the theater, come home, and go to work in the bank." And that's what he did, hoping he would become a good enough provider to get married.

In the summer of 1925, Mrs. Louis P. Aloe took three of her four daughters, including Isabel, to Europe. When they disembarked at New York in the early fall, Howard Baer was there to meet them. He took Isabel to a nightclub, and before the evening was over they were engaged.

Howard Baer and Isabel Aloe were married in St. Louis on June 26, 1926. They went to Charleston to live, but were called back to St. Louis after six months. The health of Louis P. Aloe was failing. He thought that his new son-in-law could take over the business. Baer wryly observed that he was picked because he was the only choice, being the only male in the family.

Young Baer was reluctant at first to enter his father-in-law's firm but finally agreed and started out at a salary of $6,000 a year. "I learned later," he said, "'that the company was paying me only $3,000. Mr. Aloe was paying the rest out of his own pocket.''

Aloe died in 1929 and Baer, who had had only two years to learn the business, took over the presidency.

The Aloe Company was hit hard by the depression, and the young president fought hard to keep it from going down. People who didn't have money for food didn't have money for medical care.

The company managed to stay afloat and then revived. Young Baer had shrewdly dumped the optical business and concentrated on surgical instruments. Great advances in medicine, pharmacology, and surgery began showing up in the mid-1930s. Health care was on its way to becoming the nation's fourth largest industry.

When war came, the long arm of Uncle Sam reached out and tapped Howard Baer on the shoulder. He was then forty. He left the presidency of Aloe for the duration for active duty with the army medical department in New York to oversee purchase of army medical supplies. For his efforts he received a Legion of Merit decoration. He left the army in 1945 with the rank of colonel and returned to the presidency of Aloe.

Throughout the 1950s the Aloe company continued to grow. It became "a pretty fast track," Baer said. "The pressures on me were getting heavy. The task of running the expanding company was getting bigger. I wasn't sure I could carry on much longer."

About that time the Brunswick Company of Chicago, notable for its bowling equipment and pool tables, was seeking diversification. It made an attractive offer to buy Aloe. The merger took place in 1959. Baer stayed on as Aloe division president for about a year, served on the board a while longer, and moved into the retirement he had been carefully planning. He felt a great freedom with retirement, although he continued to work for civic betterment.

The Baers had two children and enjoyed city living. Well-stocked library shelves in their home tended toward the classics. Baer was something of a philosopher, and his reading ranged from detective stories to Izaak Walton's *The Compleat Angler*. Once when Baer was publicly described as a renaissance man, he retorted that he considered himself a renaissance bum, because he knew a little about everything but not a great deal about any one thing.

Of his long career and active retirement he said, "It couldn't have worked out better. Frankly, I've had the time of my life."

Harold E. Thayer

FROM TIME TO TIME, Harold E. Thayer, head of the Mallinckrodt Chemical Works, looked out the windows of his seventh floor office and contemplated a thirty-nine-acre sprawl of time-worn industrial buildings, a few of which seemed as old as the dun-colored Mississippi River a stone's throw away.

The Mallinckrodt company looked old because it *was* old. It had started manufacturing chemicals 125 years earlier, when the thirty-nine-acre tract was a potato farm. It was a conservative family-owned company that prospered, grew at random, and moved into the mid-twentieth century looking and acting just a little old-fashioned.

By the 1960s, the venerated old firm was wallowing in the doldrums. But by 1972 it was one of the fastest growing chemical companies in the United States. The industrial activities within the rambling plant, then at Second and Mallinckrodt streets, were as modern as the atomic age which, indeed, the company historically helped to usher in.

The man behind this transformation was Harold Thayer, who was put in charge in 1960. In 1972 he was named chairman of the board of directors and chief executive officer. Thayer was direct, forthright, and unpretentious. He wasted no seconds getting down to business, because time was a valuable commodity that he hoarded.

Thayer came to St. Louis in 1939 from the East to take a minor position with the Mallinckrodt firm, and he wasn't too sure he liked the place at first. When he reached a position of power and influence as president of the company, he also turned part of his time and energy to working quietly for the betterment of the community.

St. Louis was quick to realize that Thayer was willing to lend a hand wherever needed. He became one of the most sought-after men when

there were civic or humanitarian chores that needed a high capability.

To lengthen his working day he held about four breakfast meetings a week. Then he headed for the office to start his regular day. These dawn patrol sessions won him a fame of sorts. He also used luncheons for business discussions, and after office hours he frequently attended meetings that dealt with civic activities.

His constant companion was a little black book, frequently pulled out of an inside pocket to consult. It contained telephone numbers, notations of things he must do, appointments, and other information, including a lot of birthdays, wedding anniversaries, and similar data.

"Businesslike, yes; but a very human guy who did a lot of things for people," said a friend. He drove hard, pushed himself, and expected a lot—and got a lot—out of his own employees and those he worked with on outside activities.

Like many open-hearted people who saw the needs of the community and wanted to do something to help, Harold Thayer went into the front lines in 1960 as a campaigner for the United Fund, as one of the army of 40,000 willing workers who annually went out to raise millions for the social service agencies.

His involvement in civic progress and human welfare reached new heights in 1972. He believed that culture in its various manifestations was good for a community. So he readily consented when called upon to head the campaign of the Arts and Education Fund.

He was then given a civic role of great potential. The job was president of the newly created St. Louis Regional Commerce and Growth Association. It was built on the chamber of commerce and sought to develop economically and improve an area embracing St. Louis and the seven counties adjacent to it on both sides of the Mississippi, four in Missouri and three in Illinois.

Thayer was honored by the National Conference of Christians and Jews, which annually gave awards to three outstanding St. Louisans—a Protestant, a Jew, and a Catholic.

A fervent supporter of the ideals of democracy and free enterprise, Thayer impressed those qualities on many young people in St. Louis. He worked closely with the growing generation in such sturdy institutions as the Boy Scouts, Junior Achievement, Girl Scouts, the YMCA, and others. A scout himself when young, he served three terms as president of the St. Louis Area Council of the Boy Scouts of America. He was given the Silver Beaver award for his many services to the group.

The chemical industry was big in the St. Louis area, a close third behind food and beverages. The surging growth of the Mallinckrodt firm showed convincingly that industry could thrive and increase within the city. Thayer received national recognition for his achievement as a business administrator and chemical engineer when he was given the post of chairman of the executive committee of the Manufacturing Chemists Association, a non-profit organization which embraced ninety percent of the chemical production facilities of the United States and Canada. He was also elected to a three-year term on the board of directors.

Thayer was a director of the St. Louis Research Council and a member of Civic Progress. He served as a director-at-large of the Missouri State Chamber of Commerce. He served on the advisory board of the Salvation Army; as a director, executive committee member and treasurer of the Bi-State chapter of the American Red Cross; and as a trustee of St. Luke's Hospital.

He was the director and past president of the Backstoppers, which assisted financially the bereaved widows and families of firemen and policemen killed in line of duty. He was a trustee of the Narcotics Service Council, which helped youths and adults who were in trouble with drugs, particularly those who wanted to kick the habit. He served as a member and as treasurer of the Missouri Republican finance committee from 1967 to 1969.

Thayer was a stalwart in the job pledge campaigns of 1968-70 by the National Alliance of Businessmen, metropolitan St. Louis area. He was a director of the Municipal Opera Association and a trustee of the City Art Museum.

He was a member of the board of trustees of Washington University and on the president's council of Saint Louis University. When Webster College sought a $10 million development fund, he campaigned as the primary gifts department chairman.

A measure of the esteem in which he was held as a business administrator was the number of firms on which he has served as a director. In addition to Mallinckrodt, he was on the boards of Alvey, Inc., American Air Filter Company, Inc., Carboline Company, Curlee Clothing Company, First National Bank in St. Louis, First Union, Inc., Laclede Gas Company, the Missouri Pacific Railroad Company, and General American Life Insurance Company.

Harold Eugene Thayer was born in Rochester, New York, in 1912, the only child of Herbert A. Thayer and Helen Hazels Thayer. Both parents were osteopaths. They had met during their student days at Missouri's Kirksville College of Osteopathy and Surgery.

Harold grew up in Rochester and attended Monroe High School, where he was editor-in-chief and business manager of the school paper. He was vice-president of his class and also social chairman, and he distinguished himself by winning an award for the most advancement in the Boy Scouts in a single year.

He showed exemplary industry. After school and on Saturdays he worked for an A & P grocery store for $3.75 a week. "I did everything from cleaning up the cellar to packing potatoes in bags, waiting on the customers and eating too many cookies," he remembered.

His graduating class had its dreams, and young Thayer's was: "I wanted to get a salary of $5,000 a year so I could get a Buick and belong to a country club."

But what he essentially wanted was to be "associated with business." Several universities were available to him, and his mother pushed him into Massachusetts Institute of Technology, where he could take science and learn something about business.

"I figured I was never going to win a Nobel prize in chemistry, so my studies at MIT were three-fourths chemical engineering and one-fourth business administration," he said.

To help pay expenses, he got a summer job as a traveling salesman with a Rochester firm that dealt in flower seeds, hopped in a second-hand 1929 Model A Ford, and barreled through Pennsylvania, Ohio, and Indiana.

When he graduated from MIT—"in the low section of the dean's list"—in 1934, the nation was still in the grip of the Great Depression, but young Thayer had lined up a job with the dyestuff division (Calco) of American Cyanamid in Bound Brook, New Jersey. With fourteen other new men he was put through a thorough technical sales training course and spent two years working in the company's offices, laboratories, and customers' plants. Then he got an eastern sales territory and applied his knowledge.

Through a college friend he met a secretary who worked for an advertising agency in nearby Rutherford, New Jersey. Her name was Elinor Constantinides. They dated for about a year and were married in Rutherford in 1938.

After five years Thayer concluded that he wasn't going anywhere with the dyestuff company. He was also tired of traveling so much. He got a new job through MIT and wound up at Mallinckrodt.

"I was not convinced that Mallinckrodt was a great place or that I was going to be here forever," he said. "I was interested in trying to find ways to make things happen faster."

Soon things did happen faster, and the reason was World War II.

The old-fashioned Mallinckrodt Chemical Works was destined for a rendezvous with history. Thayer, who impressed the company more than it had impressed him, moved up to become the war production board coordinator.

The company played a big role in fueling the first atomic chain reaction and subsequently the first atomic bomb. Its long expertise in the field of drug purity had caused the Manhattan Project scientists to tag Mallinckrodt for the purification of uranium. Mallinckrodt came through with exactly what the scientists wanted, bringing the world much closer to the end of that war.

For the next twenty-five years Mallinckrodt processed uranium and related materials, first for the Manhattan Project and later for the peacetime Atomic Energy Commission.

Thayer found his niche in 1943 when he was made project manager of Mallinckrodt's operations for the Manhattan Project. "I knew I had arrived at something I wanted to do," he said.

The Atomic Energy Commission was created by Congress to develop, use, and control atomic energy both for military and peaceful purposes. Mallinckrodt continued to process uranium and related materials for the AEC which eventually, in 1955, built a $65 million plant at Weldon Spring, in St. Charles County, which Mallinckrodt operated until 1967, when the plant was shut down.

Thayer managed the uranium processing project until 1952, when for three years he functioned as the company's director of development. Then he returned as project manager for the Weldon Spring operation from 1955 until 1958.

An authority in the nuclear field, in 1958 he became technical advisor to the U.S. Department of State at the second International Conference on the Peaceful Uses of Atomic Energy at Geneva, Switzerland.

In 1959 he was promoted to executive vice-president of Mallinckrodt, and the following year reached the top as president. "And I got a chance to change all the things I had been bitching about for twenty years," he commented.

The company had always made money. During the war years its profits had been impressive, but in the 1950s the firm faltered. The old, conservative family control remained in the person of Edward Mallinckrodt, Jr., son of the founder. He and his father had been the only board chairmen the company had in nearly a century. When Mallinckrodt retired in 1965 at age eighty-seven, Thayer succeeded him as the first non-family chairman.

A lone framed photograph hung on a wall of Harold Thayer's office, showing the Gateway Arch, Busch Stadium, and other progressive transformations that occurred in the downtown area as a result of a new spirit in civic leadership. It was an inspiration and encouragement to him.

"The city and county must get together. Business, labor, politicians, government and the citizenry must join for progressive action. It has been done in other cities, and it can be done here," he said.

W. L. Hadley Griffin

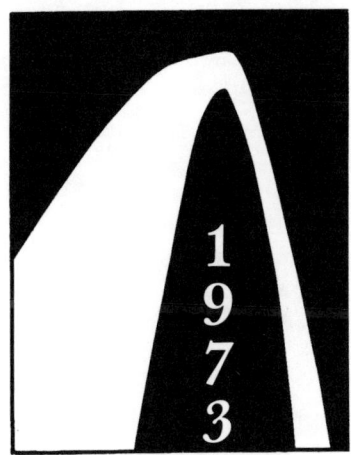

H ADLEY GRIFFIN WAS THE PRESIDENT, chief executive officer, and chairman of the board of Brown Group, Inc., a diversified corporation dealing chiefly in shoes and whose huge size could be measured by an annual report which showed enormous growth.

As is typical of most big business leaders, Hadley Griffin couldn't find enough hours in the day. He and the directors of his company added time by holding board meetings during the lunch hour. He took the stairs two at a time because he didn't want to wait for elevators.

Despite the fast pace of his life, Hadley Griffin over the years was always able to find time—his own—to do something for his fellow human beings. And he gave countless hours of hard work for the betterment of his community.

People who worked with him said that his managerial style was quiet, deliberate, and well-organized. He never raised his voice, but that didn't mean he couldn't be firm and tough when he had to be.

Those around him spoke of him as incisively analytical, innovative, and meticulously careful in his evaluations and judgments. He was sometimes called an intellectual, a student of finance and business management. He attacked problems with the discipline of a lawyer and a naval officer, both of which he was.

And then there was that other facet of his life—his dedication to the welfare of the community. "He really loves St. Louis," was often repeated by those who have known him long and well. "Doing something for it is his pride." Another said, "He's a patron of the arts because he has a genuine love for the finer things of life, not just because it is the thing to do."

Griffin simply said, "There are certain things in a community that

have to be done. They require a lot of care and a lot of work. And somebody has to do them. We can't complain about things unless we participate, unless we help make them better."

Over the years Hadley Griffin served the United Fund with willing hands. As campaign chairman in 1972, he studied the situation carefully and then gave the campaign a fresh approach and a new urgency. He set the pace himself and gave close attention to all details. Seldom had there been such personal involvement by a general campaign chairman, said many of the workers. The drive was an inspiring success.

The esteem in which Griffin was held both as a civic leader and as a business leader became manifest when he was elected to the presidency of Civic Progress. "He's a mover and shaker around town—a real power," came one comment.

When he was a boy, Hadley Griffin was a loser at trying to master a musical instrument. As a schoolboy attending Principia, he tried the bass viol. "It was found mutually desirable that the association between me and the bass viol be dissolved," he said. At the behest of his parents he next took piano lessons. He always liked music and used to take the double-decker bus to the old Odeon Theater to hear the symphony orchestra. He became one of its most ardent supporters.

He has been a rock of strength to the Arts and Education Fund and has worked to raise money for it. He began in the days when it was hard to get anyone to contribute money for culture in St. Louis and even harder to get volunteer solicitors.

Griffin is an alumnus of the Washington University School of Law and through the years has given freely of his time and effort for that educational institution. He helped raise funds for it and served it in many other ways, including as a member of its board of trustees.

Interested in youth since the time his three grown sons were young, Griffin was active in the St. Louis Area Council of the Boy Scouts. In Boy Scout circles he is remembered for his conscious determination to fulfill a speaking commitment. He had agreed to address a luncheon of Eagle Scouts. When the day came, Griffin was in the middle of an important four-day business sojourn in Washington, D.C. But he kept his promise. He flew to St. Louis for the luncheon, then immediately flew back to Washington.

In the business field, Griffin was a director of Boatmen's Bank, Boatmen's Bancshares, Inc., and Owens-Corning Fiberglass Corporation. He served as a director and past chairman of the Footwear Industries Association.

William Lester Hadley Griffin was born on May 17, 1918, in Edwardsville, Illinois, then a quiet little community about fifteen miles northeast of downtown St. Louis. His mother, Julia Hadley, had been a longtime resident of Edwardsville, and his father, Ralph D. Griffin, had come from Chicago. He was in the leather business, then joined International Shoe Company, and eventually became a banker in St. Louis.

Hadley was the youngest of four children. When it came time for him to go to school, he was sent to Principia. Among his memories of this period were two summers spent in Colorado, where he learned to love mountains and the whole outdoors. His first hero was Charles A. Lindbergh, who excited the world when he flew nonstop from New York to Paris in 1927. The nine-year-old Hadley went to Art Hill in Forest Park to watch him fly over when he returned to St. Louis. Hadley went home happy when he caught a brief glimpse of the Lone Eagle in a ticker-tape parade downtown.

After graduating from the lower school at Principia, he went to University City High School, where he made the honor society, was editor of the yearbook, and was on the track team. After graduation, he entered Williams College at Williamstown, Massachusetts.

Wanting to be a lawyer, Griffin worked toward a bachelor of arts degree. Being on the concerts committee in college increased his interest in the Saint Louis Symphony Orchestra. He graduated cum laude.

During the four summers of his college years, Griffin worked as a counselor at a boy's camp in North Carolina. During his last summer there, a friend arranged for him to take a blind date to a dance. That's how he met Phoebe Mortimer Perry, an Asheville girl who was attending college in Philadelphia.

They saw each other periodically after Griffin began Washington University School of Law, although separated by distance. Near the end of 1941 they became engaged. And on April 1, 1942, while the world was in the turmoil of war, they were married.

After finishing the first of his required three years of law school, Hadley joined the navy. He was given intensive training to become an antisubmarine officer on a destroyer. He had the rank of lieutenant commander when the war ended.

After his discharge in September 1945, he hurried home. His first son had been born earlier, and his second would be along in a few months. He was just in time to enroll in the fall semester at Washington University and begin his final two years of law.

After he passed the bar, he decided he wanted to join a corporation, not fight courtroom battles. He quickly had an offer from a good company and while he was thinking it over, an old friend then in personnel asked him if he would be interested in joining Wohl Shoe Company, a St. Louis firm that retailed shoes through a vast number of outlets. It was headed by David P. Wohl, noted humanitarian and philanthropist.

Griffin moved into an office at the Wohl Company as its only lawyer. While he was handling the company's legal details, his receptive mind was absorbing the shoe business around him. He learned so much about management and finance that in 1950 he was made assistant secretary and treasurer.

Then, at thirty-three with a family of three sons, he was called back into active navy service for the Korean War. He was made an executive officer of the destroyer *U.S.S. Black*. The *Black* operated in the Caribbean and off the West Coast during the eighteen months he was in active service. He was released in December 1952.

Griffin picked up the raveled threads of his civilian job as a law counselor, this time for Brown Shoe Company. He had been there only a year when he was made secretary. In 1961 he was made a director and was given the title of vice-president in 1964.

The number one man in the company then was Monte E. Shomaker, whom Griffin admired. He had also admired the earlier president, Clark R. Gamble. When the Brown Shoe treasurer died in 1964, Griffin was made treasurer. Two years later he became executive vice-president.

In 1968 Griffin was made president of Brown Shoe Company, the parent of the cluster of companies that had been gathered together. He was only the fifth president the company had had in the ninety years of its existence.

A year later he became chief executive officer as well as president. In 1971 he was made chairman of the executive committee and at the beginning of 1972, when Brown Shoe, Wohl, and other companies were reorganized as Brown Group, Inc., Hadley Griffin was made chairman of the board of directors.

Under the presidency of Hadley Griffin the company moved steadily forward in sales and earnings. Griffin looked around the community he loved so well and saw that St. Louis was starting to move ahead. He believed its energies should be focused on objectives which would strengthen the economic and employment base of the region and "conserve what we already have as a foundation on which to build."

"The importance of jobs to the region's economic future means we should give the highest priority to acquiring new industry, while at the same time encouraging development of existing assets," he said.

"The fact that the private and public sectors have begun to work together more effectively should speed up such vital projects as the establishment of a St. Louis area council of governments and the expansion of one of our region's great assets, the Port of St. Louis.''

Lawrence K. Roos

AT A TIME WHEN Americans were becoming increasingly disillusioned by malodorous government and political chicanery, Lawrence K. Roos showed St. Louis County that an administration could serve the people for twelve years without a scent of scandal. He demonstrated that the American system can work and that one county government was able to serve its citizens honestly, efficiently, and effectively.

When Larry Roos began his first campaign in 1962, he was not well known to the voters of St. Louis County. Indeed, the office of county supervisor, which he sought, was not particularly attractive. When he left office in 1974, his face was as familiar as the kitchen stove and the office of supervisor was very prestigious. Roos came to be regarded as the dominant governmental figure in the St. Louis region.

Larry Roos came to government as a solid, successful banker who had a knack for tough business management. He owned controlling interests in two small banks which, in response to the aggressive and progressive policies he instituted, were growing and prospering.

Shortly out of Yale, he served three and a half years with the army in Europe during World War II, was decorated, and advanced from private to major on merit. He came out of the war with some ideals about the commonweal. He was civic-minded, believed that the welfare of the community depended on good, honest government, and that able private citizens should not leave rule to the professional politicians and party hacks. He was chairman of a Missouri citizens' committee which campaigned in behalf of presidential candidate Dwight D. Eisenhower.

But running for public office was far from his mind on a cold day in January 1962 when he met with three old friends. The government needed able new leadership and guidance, they told him. Would he,

respected businessman and civic leader, run for county supervisor on the Republican ticket?

The prospect excited Roos. He consulted with his wife, Mary. She agreed. Recalling the day of his acceptance of the challenge, he said, "I have always felt that the survival of our American system of government depends on strong local government at the grass roots level. I could not conceive of any better place to put that theory to work than in St. Louis County."

His modernization and streamlining of county government and the efficiency and integrity of its operation made St. Louis County recognized nationally as one of the best managed political subdivisions in the nation.

Lawrence Kalten Roos was born on February 1, 1918, on McPherson Avenue in St. Louis. His parents were Sol and Selma Roos. Sol Roos was a self-made man. He had been born in Germany, came to America when he was seventeen, got a job with a metal company, and rose to the top. He was a reserved man who maintained the kind of German discipline which kept his son on his toes.

Larry attended Country Day School. His father pored over his report cards meticulously and made known his displeasure when they were unsatisfactory. After graduation from Country Day, Larry went to Yale University, where he took a liberal arts course. "I majored in modern European history which helped me in nothing," he said.

Young Roos was beset by shyness during his school years. He was, he said frankly, an introvert. He remembered that he dreaded to make speeches. Because of his introversion, he did not participate in student activities. He never sought class offices; he was no leader. "I wasn't a big man on campus," he said. "I was a small man on campus. You can look in my school yearbook and you will find no boy of distinction there, no mention of my being the one most likely to succeed."

Throughout his school years he had no well-defined idea of what he wanted to do when the time came for him to go out into the world. He was still uncertain when he graduated from Yale in June 1940.

Back in St. Louis after graduation, Roos took a job with an electric company. This was interrupted in June 1941 when he was drafted into the army, about six months before Pearl Harbor. His early association with the army was not inspiring. Three months of basic training were made more difficult by a sergeant who disliked the erudite Yale graduate. "I served more KP than anyone else," Roos remembered.

He spent a year at Camp Polk, got involved in signal communications, and was commissioned a second lieutenant. He was ordered to northern Ireland to train at an amphibious school for an African landing. Then he was sent to General Eisenhower's headquarters in London. Later he was transferred to Gen. Omar Bradley's First Army Group headquarters in London, which was then involved in planning the Normandy invasion. Roos had risen to captain and was doing staff work in signal communications. Early in June 1944 he moved onto the European continent with the successful Normandy invasion. He came home in 1945 with the Bronze Star and five battle stars.

Back home and in civilian clothes again, he still had the problem of what he was going to do with himself. He accepted an offer to join Westheimer & Company, an advertising and public relations firm in downtown St. Louis. During the next three years he picked up knowledge and experience that would be useful to him later in his banking and political careers.

Shortly after becoming a civilian, he was having lunch and a gripe session with friends. Arthur Freund asked, "Why don't you get into politics and do something about the things you don't like?"

The idea clung to his mind. He decided to seek a seat in the Missouri House of Representatives and filed as a Republican in the primary. He won in the general election and became the youngest member of the Missouri legislature during his first term.

Roos established a fine legislative record over two terms and made a name for himself by making life miserable for the small loan lobby in Jefferson City. At the end of four years in the legislature, he settled on pursuing a business career.

With the help of his father, he was able to buy a controlling interest in the Mound City Trust Company. It was a small, solid bank which seemed to be going nowhere. Roos gave it aggressive management. He doubled the assets of the bank, making it highly successful in all operations. He then bought a controlling interest in the Security Bank of Kirkwood and gave it the same magic touch.

His success as a banker served two purposes, he said. "I achieved a significant financial success; and I was able to prove that my success was not the result of being the son of a wealthy father."

During the next dozen years he became a respected banker. He acted like a banker and looked like a banker, wearing dark suits. He emerged as a civic leader, taking part in philanthropies. And he kept a hand in politics, being a delegate to the Republican National Convention in 1956.

His interests expanded. He was Missouri chairman of the Crusade for Freedom and traveled overseas to observe the operation of Radio Free Europe. He was treasurer of the executive committee of the Greater St. Louis United Fund. He was on the boards of the Central Institute for the Deaf, Jewish Hospital, and the Jewish Community Centers Association. He was president of the Wesley House Association, vice-president of the St. Louis-St. Louis County Associated Bankers, a member of the board of advisors of the Ninth Region Small Business Association, and a member of the board of trustees of Country Day School.

He also became a married man. A year or so after he returned from the war, Larry Roos, then twenty-eight, married Harriet Rosenberg, a St. Louisan. Two children were born to them, Mary Ellen and Lawrence K. (Chip). The marriage ended in divorce in 1953. In April 1955 he married Mary Watson Ross, a St. Louis widow.

When Roos was elected county supervisor in 1962, one of his first acts was to sell his holdings in his two banks to avoid any possibility of a conflict of interest. His salary as supervisor—$10,000 a year—was less than half of that of the mayor of the city of St. Louis.

In some uncanny way, Roos found people of rare executive ability for the key positions of his government. He eliminated hundreds of useless jobs, reformed purchasing practices, introduced swift, accurate data processing in keeping records and files. A paramount achievement of his administration was his persuasion of the voters to update the county government by adoption of a new charter in 1968 that permitted modernization of the governmental structure through sweeping organizational changes. This was followed by home rule, which at long last gave Missouri's largest political entity the right to conduct its own affairs.

The dependability, honesty, and effectiveness of the Roos administration so well earned the trust of the voters that they passed five bond issues which provided funds to build highways, parks, public buildings, and other improvements. A new county government center materialized in Clayton, a complex of three buildings and a plaza, recognized as one of the most modern seats of county government in the nation.

The never-ending war on crime was stepped up by Supervisor Roos, who increased the county police force from 132 to 540. The department was reorganized and professionalized, a police crime laboratory was established, police helicopter service was inaugurated, and the county began training its policemen in the Metropolitan Police Training Academy.

Major facilities and new expanded services were added to the St. Louis County Hospital and Health Department. New clinics were opened and a mobile health clinic was put in operation.

Meanwhile, the hardworking supervisor carried on an enduring fight against blight, housing evils, air pollution, and drug abuse. He developed programs to reduce juvenile delinquency. His popularity mounted and he became a man who seemed invincible at the polls.

In 1968 he was unwisely prevailed upon to run for governor against Warren E. Hearnes. Roos made a valiant campaign, but Hearnes was at the height of his popularity and buried the county supervisor under an avalanche of votes.

Roos made county government responsive to the people. He brought better cooperation between the unincorporated part of the county the ninety-three incorporated municipalities, then moved toward alleviating the political fragmentation that weakened the county. Looking into the future, he did not believe the day would come when the incorporated municipalities in the county would cease to exist, but he thought that small towns would be eliminated and large municipalities would exist on a partnership basis with the county government.

Roos was an ardent supporter of regional cooperation. "I don't think that St. Louis City and St. Louis County will ever merge," he said, "but I do think they can cooperate over a wide area."

Colleagues in his administration described Roos as a bundle of energy, a man dedicated to his job, a man who knew no limit on working hours. Another described his administration as "twelve years of hard work and dedication to the county. He has brought the county up to its highest point." Roos was seen as a "very warm person" with a great sense of humor. But he could be tough. "He got one hell of a lot of work out of his staff," an associate said.

Edwin S. Jones

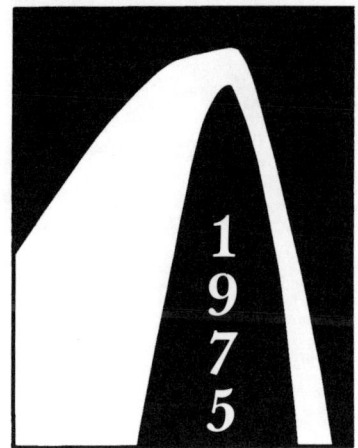

EDWIN S. JONES WORKED in the gilt-edged world of the executive suite, but he once stitched men's shirts in a factory sewing room to learn more about the dry goods business. He was a civic catalyst in banker's gray, a mover of monetary and municipal mountains who for many years donned a red suit and beard to play Santa Claus to cancer patients.

He was a churchman, a clubman, a civic patriot. He's been known as Mr. Fixit, a woodworker, a Sunday school teacher, and a bomber pilot who later flew his own plane around the state.

This was Edwin Scoville Jones, former chairman of the board of the First National Bank in St. Louis, chairman and chief executive officer of First Union, Inc., involved citizen in corporate, cultural, collegiate, and charitable St. Louis.

A son of Yale and alumnus of Country Day School, he was as informal as his nickname—Ted—used alike by family and friends, childhood chums, corporate colleagues, and just about everybody in the bank.

Yet his informality was cloaked with dignity, a mix of grave courtesy, quiet, dry humor, old-fashioned conservatism and new-breed audacity. Despite his British heritage—his father came here from England—and despite working in the heady climate of high finance, his voice and his views reflected the tone and timber of middle America.

Jones was a low-profile activist, an unpretentious executive as quietly genial as the neighborhood druggist. He was a pragmatic visionary, a low-key, long-range thinker and planner.

Jones was a director of Alton Box Board Co., Angelica Corp., Anheuser-Busch, First National Bank in St. Louis, First Union, General American Life Insurance Company, General Steel Industries, Interco, McDonnell Douglas, McDonnell Douglas Finance Corp., Southwestern

Bell Telephone Company, Union Electric, and Vico Corp. He was a president of Civic Progress, a president of the chamber of commerce and its outgrowth organization, the St. Louis Regional Commerce and Growth Association. He was also a board member of the Civic Center Redevelopment Corporation. He was president of the United Way several years ago and was general chairman of an over-the-top campaign.

He was an officer, director, or working member of the Barnard Free Skin and Cancer Hospital, Boy Scouts, YMCA, Junior Achievement, Municipal Theater, educational television, St. Louis Art Museum, Missouri Public Expenditure Survey, Reserve City Bankers Association, American Bankers Association, American Institute of Banking, and Association of Bank Holding Companies. He was a trustee of Washington University and on the president's council of Saint Louis University.

But Jones was not one to lend his name and forget where he put it. He gave it outright, along with his time. As United Way chairman, he visited many member agencies and, both as chairman and president, he missed few, if any, meetings of the campaign troops.

As Gen. Leif J. Sverdrup said of him, "He never pushes himself. He does a tremendous job without anyone ever knowing anything about it. He's always in there. Civic Progress or whatever the job, he's in there working and getting the job done."

"Ted Jones is a working board member," said August A. Busch III. "You can depend on his advice. One of his best traits in my opinion, is that he never concentrates power around himself. He knows how to delegate authority and responsibility into every organization."

"He's sedate and serious," said George M. Capps, "but I've seen him get up at a party and do a soft shoe routine. Hope writes songs—she's very talented—and they may get up and sing."

Hope is Mrs. Jones, the former Hope Virginia DePew, a member of a prominent St. Louis family and a warmly hospitable hostess.

Just as Jones' public and civic lifestyles were fragmented, so his private world was a mosaic of the social, the serene, and the simple. It might have been the white-tie-and-tails world of the Veiled Prophet's ball, where their daughter, Hope Florence Jones, was crowned Queen of Love and Beauty in her debut year of 1972.

It might have been the slacks-and-shirt-sleeves world of a rare evening at home, reading financial publications in the library before an open fire, making a model engine, repairing a chair or crafting with skill a piece of furniture in the downstairs workshop. It might have been the rough-hewn world of the outdoorsman, hunting in nearby woods or fishing in the wilds of Canada with his family.

It is likely, though, no matter how remote or peaceful the region, he was thinking about St. Louis' problems and their solutions. His love affair with his native city began in boyhood, grew while he was away at college and at war, and was enhanced when he later sought—but never found—a place where he'd rather settle down.

"I think St. Louis is just about ideal," he said. "I like its size. I like the people. I think it has a great future. We've had a hard time getting it turned around, but how can it miss?

"Here we are in the middle of the United States, on the biggest river, at the hub of everything. Someday, we'll get our problems straightened out and then we're really going to be in the forefront of the country's major metropolitan centers.

"Like every city in this part of the country, we've had problems getting labor pulling together with management. We've had racial changes because of our geographical location. But I think we've been fairly successful. We're trying our best to improve housing and education and health care and crime prevention and all the other things that make up a good, healthy community.

"Education, health care, and housing are the three most important areas that are not in very good shape. The city school system is in bad shape. In housing we've had probably the most visible disaster in any major city, Pruitt-Igoe. We know that concept failed, and I hope we won't repeat this mistake."

Ted Jones was the youngest of the six children of Mr. and Mrs. C. Norman Jones. His father was in the brewery business, and after Prohibition he was chairman of Title Insurance Company. Ted had four brothers: Herbert, a builder; Lawrence, in business in Texas; Richard; and D. Calhoun Jones. His sister is Mrs. Carl Lischer.

"We had a great home life, although there was a big difference in age between my eldest brother and me. In those days family life was different. You fell into the pattern of things and accepted it and didn't question values and purposes and philosophies the way children do today."

Ted graduated from Country Day School in 1934, then entered Yale. Two years later he left New Haven to return to St. Louis, taking a stock clerk's job with Ely & Walker, a major wholesale dry goods firm.

It was a natural starting place. His grandfather, David R. Calhoun, Sr., had been president of the firm. E. P. Cave was then president and David R. Calhoun, Jr., was vice president. This would be the first of many times that the business, civic, and philanthropic paths of Ted Jones and David Calhoun would cross, the first of many times Jones would follow in his older relative's footsteps. Both men had dropped out of college to go into the business world.

"We were still feeling the effects of the depression," said Jones, "and I thought I was somewhat of a financial burden on my family. I figured I had had two good years at college and since I knew I would have to go to work anyway, I thought I would go that much earlier and get a jump on the others.

"What I learned was hardly an education in business and finance, but it was an education in hard work. I started as a stock clerk, opened up bales of piece goods, and put them on the counter. Then I became an order-filler and that was a big day. My salary went up to fifty-five bucks a month.

"Those experiences were really great and I wouldn't trade them for anything. Some of the work was hard. It was strictly manual labor, but I had an opportunity to learn, and I did my best to learn. I studied the difference between the qualities of the piece goods, the thread counts and weights. When I got through that, they made me a salesman, but I didn't get many accounts because I was the youngest and newest.

"I went into factories to learn how things were made. That's how I learned to sew. I went into a shirt factory in Kennett, Missouri, and had a chance to learn all the special operations. I would cut out the pieces and sew them together, and hopefully it would end up as a shirt. I was at a sewing machine in a room with 300 women, the only man."

Jones was still at Ely & Walker when World War II became imminent and he decided to learn to fly. Starting his training in 1939, he went into the Civilian Pilot Training Program, the Civil Air Patrol, the U.S. Navy, and finally into the Army Air Corps. He flew thirty missions over Europe, most as a first pilot with his own squadron.

At war's end, the two most important events in his life occurred for the handsome young captain. He married a hometown girl and he changed jobs.

He had known Hope when they were growing up in St. Louis, but they didn't date seriously until his return from service. On November 30, 1946, they were married in the Church of St. Michael and St. George.

On January 2 of the same year, Jones began his banking career with tasks almost as humble as those assigned him earlier at Ely & Walker.

"At Yale I was majoring in economics and was interested in finance. I assumed I would go into business, but actually, I had never thought much about banking. When I got out of the service, although they were kind enough to offer me my old job, I decided I didn't want to go back to Ely & Walker.

"I had traveled around the country, trying to find a challenge, then came back to St. Louis and someone suggested I think about First National. I didn't have much interest, but when I went to the bank and saw that so many of the officers were way up in years, I felt there would be an opportunity there."

His observations were prophetic. He did find his opportunity at First National and was a vice president in 1955 when his old company, Ely & Walker, was sold to Burlington Industries of North Carolina.

Jones' official biography fleshes out his career with specific dates: January 1962, executive vice-president and member of the advisory board; December 1968, president and member of the board of directors; March 1970, chairman of the board and chief executive officer (relinquishing the title of CEO in March 1974); April 1971, president and chief operating officer of First Union, Inc; April 1972, chief executive officer; March 1973, chairman of the board.

Those who watched him deal with a myriad of matters every day agreed that he was never frustrated or frantic, although he admitted sometimes to getting a little excited. Why did he take on so many unpaid jobs to help the community?

"I have lived here all my life," he answered. "This community has been good to me. I want it to flourish. I'm proud of it. If you want to get, you have to give. Nothing will happen unless you give your time and money and support."

Does he think the American city is doomed because of the horrendous expense of municipal services and a dwindling tax base?

"There are signs that this is happening," he conceded. "Certainly, St. Louis is not alone in facing this unsolved problem.

"How are we going to solve such things as transportation and housing and crime prevention and education and jobs and provide services that must exist in order to have a healthy community? If you ask me for a master plan, I don't have one.

"But I do believe it's going to take a lot of rethinking on the part of city and government leaders. It's going to take a lot of rethinking on the part of citizens. If they want these things, they have to be willing to turn over more of their income to underwriting the cost.

"On the other hand"—and Jones, in a rare display of emphasis, banged his fist on the desk—"city officials are going to have to produce a more efficient operation."

George H. Capps

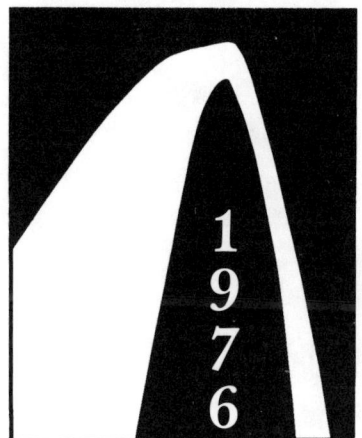

GEORGE HOWARD CAPPS leaped through life non-stop, a work-happy whirling dervish of the briefcase set, the Grand Prix champion of the executive suite.

Capps was a patriot without a party label, a free-enterpriser and adamant capitalist who ached for the underdog, a staunch conservative with a rebel touch.

He ran a worldwide conglomerate that stretched from St. Louis to Hong Kong with the skill and savvy of the boardroom and genial gusto of an ice cream social. But with all his work, he never really left the warm and special world he shared with Helen Capps and their family of seven.

George Capps' achievements, as well as the pace of his daily schedule, were almost overwhelming: An ex-navy man, former FBI agent, ex-judo instructor, Eagle Scout, political campaign fundraiser, and sports event promoter, commercial developer, property buyer and seller, builder, transporter, investor, merchant, financier, corporate executive, board member, and international industrial magnate whose interests ranged from cars to coal, from land to leasing, from fine gems to barge lines, insurance to restaurants, auto freight to motels. And he was a civic leader, community worker, and volunteer for charitable projects.

In his twenty-five-year climb from selling coal to heading a conglomerate, Capps moved swiftly into the boardroom and executive suite and into the rarefied climate of civic leadership. He was on seventeen corporate, community, hospital, university, and agency boards, and was frequently cited for community service, leadership in promoting harmonious human relations, and business acumen.

From boyhood in his native St. Louis, Capps set goals and met them.

Born into the warm, affectionate family circle of coal company president George A. Capps, he grew out of a childhood bout with allergies into a self-professed "health nut," with a gym in his basement, a swimming pool and tennis court in the backyard, and a closet full of vitamins.

As an Eagle Scout, Capps earned fifty-four merit badges, third highest in the area, and he never lost his enthusiasm for the organization. In 1973 he was awarded the Distinguished Eagle Award.

In his effervescent enthusiasm for anything yet untried, in the summer of 1934 he snatched the chance to sell telephone service for Southwestern Bell—not realizing that he would someday sit on that utility's board—and he worked so persistently that he earned up to $100 a week, many times the average man's wages in those dark depression days.

He picked up more than a paycheck. He learned what people wanted. "I would ring doorbells from early morning until dinnertime, then go back for follow-up calls in the evening when the husbands were home," he reminisced. If he felt a family really couldn't afford it, he wouldn't try to sell them. Instead, he would go around the neighborhood collecting things the family needed.

This was the youth who grew up to become chairman of the Cardinal Glennon Memorial Hospital board, president of the Backstoppers, board member of the Child Care Center of Our Lady of Grace, campaign chairman and later president of the United Way. He was also the men's chairman of the first Camelot auction.

A graduate of Washington University, where he was an active fraternity man, associate editor and business manager of the yearbook, and business manager of the newspaper, Capps stayed on the hill to obtain his law degree. But, he admitted with a laugh, the legal world was not for him.

The approach of World War II opened the escape hatch and ultimately led Capps back into industry. With boyhood friends he enlisted in the navy in October 1940 and served aboard the *U.S.S. Arkansas*.

In law school he had become so interested in the FBI that he had applied to be an agent. They were very much interested, but said he would have to wait until he was twenty-five. However, the FBI called back a year early, and Capps was quickly detached from navy service and sent to Washington. That telephone call was to change not only his career, but his life.

For also working at FBI headquarters was a pretty blonde girl from Minnesota, Helen B. Schulte, who would become his wife. "I only dated her five weeks before I was sent overseas on special assignment," Capps reported, "but when I came back a year later we were married."

"Really," Capps said of his life, "the strong point has been my family. The kids are extraordinary. They believe in the work ethic, were excellent students, and are doing a tremendous job."

It was because of his growing family and his dreams for them—along with an awareness of marketing potential overseas gained during his FBI duty tours—that Capps left the agency in 1950 to return to the family coal business. Among his FBI assignments were Dallas, San Francisco, Detroit, Salt Lake City, Reno, Washington, D.C., St. Louis, three overseas assignments, and the founding session of the United Nations.

Back in the business world things were tough for a while. "I knocked on doors all over the world for two years until I sold my first cargo," he remembered. It was 4,500 tons of coal to Mitsubishi Chemical in Japan, less than one-twentieth the size of a normal shipment today.

But it was a start, and for a period beginning in 1955, Capitol Coal and Coke was the second largest coal exporting firm in the country. Capps was traveling frequently to Europe, the Far East, and South America, marketing coal to Japanese steel plants, gas plants, European electric plants, and the Argentine railroad.

"In 1961 the coal business was so bad," he said, "that I was working twelve or fourteen hours a day, making dozens of calls, but getting no business. I couldn't stand that. So I looked for something else."

Never one to miss a chance, Capps had observed that the ships scheduled to take his coal to Europe were arriving here with import cars, and he was struck by the potential business in foreign automobiles. When one of fourteen Volkswagen distributorships in the country was offered him, he snapped it up.

That in turn led to the formation of his own truck line to deliver the cars more economically to dealers' showrooms. Like a quickly spreading stream, the infant conglomerate began to form and to absorb subsidiaries, partnerships, syndicates, joint ventures. There were more than fifty on the list.

"It was Capps who persuaded me to build Neiman-Marcus at Plaza Frontenac," Stanley Marcus said at the dedication. "He never stopped talking about the assets of St. Louis."

Despite his business commitments, Capps found time for extraordinary community service which provided neither paycheck nor profit and for the little things that few outsiders knew about.

He received the annual Brotherhood Award from the National Council of Christians and Jews, was honored by the National Jewish Hospital and Research Center in Denver, and was given, among other honors, the St. George award presented to a Catholic layman active in adult scouting, and the Executive of the Year award.

Capps was an active trustee of Washington University. He was also on the president's council of Saint Louis University and for years gave much of his time to the Backstoppers, a civic group which renders financial aid to families of area police and firemen killed in the line of duty.

An ardent patriot, intensely interested in government, he worked for both Democratic and Republican candidates. In 1953 he and Sidney Salomon, Jr., were co-chairmen of the finance committee for Raymond R. Tucker's campaign for mayor. In 1972 he was finance chairman for John C. Danforth's campaign for attorney-general.

"He is absolutely the greatest," said Danforth of Capps. "He's a man of intense energy and drive, totally selfless, absolutely committed to his family and his community. Next to my grandfather, he is the most effective man I've known."

Danforth's words were echoed by others, including his brother, Chancellor William H. Danforth of Washington University, who called Capps a "dynamo," with a "desire to see what he can do to uplift humanity."

"If we start thinking about what's wonderful about America," Capps once wrote, "it must start with our religious faith. A nation not believing in the Eternal Father of us all is a nation which cannot long endure. I hope we will always love our country, as it deserves to be held high and revered and respected."

To his fellow St. Louisans, he would say, "St. Louis' main thrust should be to bring industry into the area. In order to do this, it is necessary to sell the city and create a pro-business image. We have to sell the city on the fact that we have an extremely good labor pool, centrally located with excellent river transportation, rail transportation, truck transportation, and an unlimited source of energy across the river."

The dedicated free-enterpriser went on: "Why should business have a black eye in our society? Without business there wouldn't be money for hospitals, universities, or welfare programs. If everyone who criticizes business today would just get exposed it, he would be hooked for life." Just like George Capps.

George Capps died on September 1, 1988.

William H. Danforth

IT HAPPENED A LONG TIME AGO, but the memory of a little boy now grown to manhood stays green.

The boy and his grandfather, for whom he was named, were talking together, and the conversation turned to a certain word, a word the older man scorned. He asked the twelve-year-old to look it up in his dictionary, then to bring a pair of scissors. Together, they clipped out the offending word and threw it away.

Dr. William H. Danforth seldom, if ever, used that word. It seemed to have been cut out of his vocabulary, as well as out of the dictionary. The word: "impossible."

But then his grandfather, William H. Danforth, and in turn, his father, Donald Danforth, gave him other words to take its place. Words with muscle and teeth and backbone. Upbeat words, they were, with power:

"I dare you to!"

"Stand tall, think tall, smile tall, live tall."

Along with his name, they were his special inheritance. Products of another age, a simpler time, when a man had his heroes, and mottoes could be his lodestars, staying with him through his life.

Dr. William H. Danforth strode tall through his many worlds, taking life as a dare—as chancellor of Washington University, as an educator and administrator; as a physician and teacher and author of scientific papers; as a medical scientist as much at home in the laboratory as in the midst of a lively campus; as a community leader, a corporate director, as trustee, an active and concerned participant in the educational, business, and charitable leadership of the St. Louis area.

Scion of a distinguished St. Louis family—his late grandfather founded Ralston Purina Company, and his father built it into a worldwide

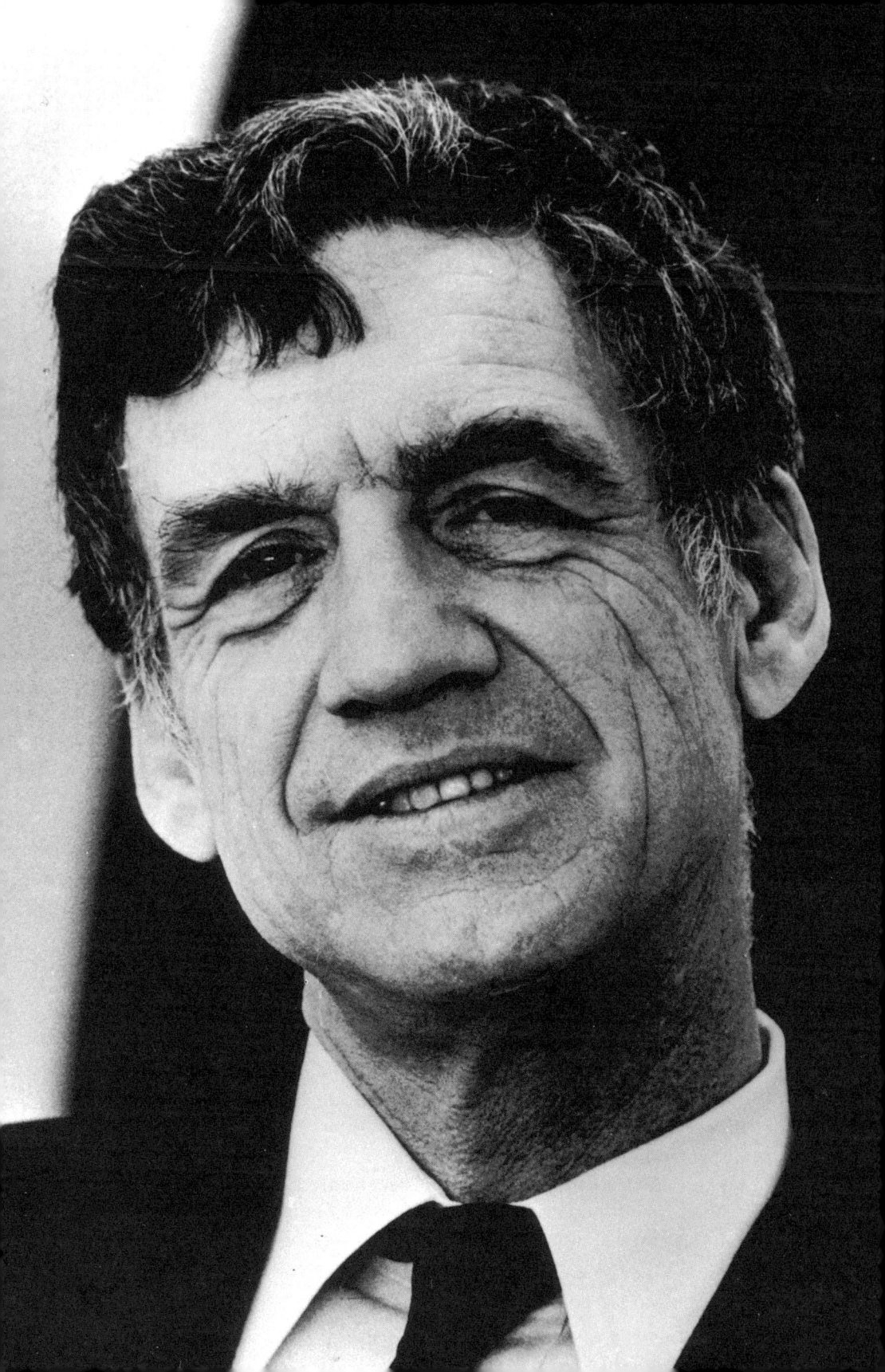

industry—he has been chairman of the board of the Danforth Foundation, chairman of the St. Louis Christmas Carols Association, and a trustee of the American Youth Foundation—all philanthropies and community activities initiated by the first William H. Danforth and carried on with enthusiasm and generosity by the family.

After one year's study at Westminster College and graduation from Princeton University in 1947, Danforth received his medical degree from Harvard in 1951 and returned to his native St. Louis to begin what he believed would a lifelong career as a practicing physician, teacher, and researcher.

But healing, he discovered, was not restricted to sick room and scalpel. As a doctor, he became nationally recognized. Once he received a congratulatory telegram from President Lyndon B. Johnson, citing his leadership of a Health and Welfare Council study committee, which expedited the passage of Medicaid legislation in Missouri.

In one of the pioneer cooperative efforts between the city's two major medical schools, Saint Louis and Washington universities, Danforth and Dr. Robert H. Felix, then dean of the Saint Louis University Medical School, organized and co-directed the Bi-State Regional Medical Program to improve health care throughout the area.

"Bill Danforth is rock solid," said W. L. Hadley Griffin, one-time chairman of the board of the Brown Group, with whom he served in the U.S. Navy during the Korean conflict. "He is smart—but he's also wise," continued Griffin. "There is a quiet powerfulness about him that makes people trust him instinctively."

The chancellor, friends at Washington University insisted, asked nothing for himself, but not even the sky was the limit for whatever cause captured his mind and heart. Even then, however, the bass voice was cushioned with courtesy. No one ever heard him yell, except for the Battling Bears of Washington University.

"I first met him," said provost Dr. Merle Kling, "when I was dean of arts and sciences and he was vice chancellor for medical affairs. There were times when the interests of arts and sciences and the medical school conflicted, and he became an adversary, a very formidable one."

"But I soon learned to respect him. Some call him a man of steel, but that doesn't capture the enormous compassion and deep concern with performing acts of kindness, not only without credit, but also unknown often to the beneficiary."

Danforth emerged in his portrait as a muted trumpet song instead of a blare, a muffled cheer instead of a raucous yell. He often worked in sweater and slacks or shirt sleeves, but he wore his Washington University tie with all the loyalty and aplomb with which his doughty grandfather donned the checkerboard cravat which was the symbol of his fledgling business empire.

To Danforth, there was no lovelier sound than the music of holiday carols. The carol-singing custom was begun many years ago by his grandfather, and the youngest member of the group each year is privileged to carry the Christmas Carols Association canister, with contributions earmarked for children's agencies.

"Bill loves Christmas carols," says his brother, Senator John C. Danforth, with a laugh, "but he can't sing a note." The senator amiably confessed he's no Caruso either, but "Bill is reputed to be the worst singer of the whole family."

Laughter came easily to the close-knit family that included brother Donald, founder and president of Danforth Agri-Resources, Inc., and Dorothy Danforth Miller, as well as the senator.

Born in St. Louis on April 10, 1926, Danforth was educated at Community School and Country Day before going on to Westminster College and Princeton. "In our home, expectations were high," Danforth said, "but discipline was rarely used. I think our family tried to instill in the children a loyalty to the family, which was a part of one's loyalty to the wider community. We were taught self-reliance, but also the sense of responsibility for one's fellows, especially for those who for some reason could not themselves be self-reliant.

"While I was growing up, I never heard my father say a negative word about any person or any group. I remember when I was about fourteen when I learned from my mother that there was someone my father didn't like. I could hardly believe it. I thought he liked everyone.

"In my family were a sense of values and a concern for others. My father and grandfather saw life as an adventure. There was the chance to accomplish something that would be lasting and would leave the world a better place. Slogans and stories were parts of our lives."

His words were underlined by Elizabeth (Ibby) Danforth, who married him in 1951, his last year of medical school. "He is a man who believes absolutely in the simple virtues," she said. "He believes that people are basically good. Often, he came home to tell me he had found a new hero or a new heroine."

That hero or heroine might be a scientist of substance and stature, a man such as Dr. Carl F. Cori, the Nobel Prize-winning biochemist, with whom Danforth worked as a young doctor and "from whom I learned that high quality research was as different from some of the things I had known and read as was a painting by Rembrandt from a child's drawing."

It may be a community and business leader, such as J. S. McDonnell, former chairman of the board of McDonnell Douglas Corporation, "who had a profound influence on my life. No one was more brilliant or far-seeing, no one provided more inspiration to others."

"When any of the four children was in the hospital," said Ibby Danforth, "Bill would just borrow a stethoscope and go right into the room and check things for himself. The most touching moment of our marriage was when daughter Beth was having open heart surgery; when she was being taken into the operating room I glanced up and saw a tear in his eye and then I just fell apart myself."

Never a stern disciplinarian, Danforth, like his father before him, was a "reasoner," not a punisher. Vacations with the children took the Danforths to the American Youth Foundation's Camp Miniwanca—he called it a very special place for the family, "a touchstone to our inner selves"— or to a Missouri river for a float trip or the Colorado mountains for skiing.

It was his respect for learning and hunger for new knowledge, coupled with the need for a challenge, that inspired Danforth first to enter medical school and, in his mid-forties to step into a brand new career as an educator-administrator. As much as he loved the second, he never forgot the first.

"It is a great privilege to be a physician," he said. "No one can go through this kind of experience without having a deepened understanding of one's fellow human beings, their hopes, their strengths, their fragilities, and especially, the common humanity that all share. Medicine is one field where you don't have to get up in the morning and wonder if you will do something good today. Your job is to do good, to relieve human suffering, and to make the world a better place to live."

"I couldn't be chancellor of Washington University if I weren't an optimist," he once declared. "You have to have faith in people, you have to believe that knowledge is better than ignorance and that human beings can learn and pass on some of what has been learned plus some accumulated wisdom to oncoming generations so that each generation can be better than the past, and we won't go on repeating mistakes over and over again.

"Being on a university campus," he continued, "seeing the student generations replace each other each time with new individuals of talent, energy, moral sensitivity, of commitment to things greater than themselves is to know that such faith is not misplaced.

"It's an exciting time to be young. There are enormous opportunities to use new-found knowledge, understanding and technology to make the world a better place. We can certainly goof it up, but we don't have to."

As he talked, the listener felt what he meant was that nothing was impossible. He didn't say it exactly that way, because the word just wasn't in his vocabulary.

Armand C. Stalnaker

Something within him didn't like a wall. Long ago this boy climbed the mountains of his Appalachian home to discover a world wide and free on the other side. Early in his youth he learned the contentment and adventure of sailing his boat against the wind in the freedom of the open waters.

Later, as a civic leader, his community stretched far beyond a city's legal limits to embrace a region of people working together. And as a businessman, his office had sweeps of glass looking beyond the concrete canyons to the horizons, an office without doors to shut people out, without a desk to build an invisible barrier.

That office was the executive heart of General American Life Insurance Company, the working world of its chairman and president, Armand C. Stalnaker.

Stalnaker didn't sit behind a massive mahogany desk. That hallowed hallmark of authority was to him a wall between himself and others. He worked instead at a round table, some five feet in diameter, its top cleared of all but the papers essential to the moment and a grouping of informal family photographs. Chairs were drawn up to the table for guests or associates.

Stalnaker's climb to the top rung of the management ladder was as orderly and steady as the man himself. He joined General American in 1963 as administrative vice-president. In 1965 he was named executive vice-president; in 1969, president and chief administrative officer; in 1973, president and chief executive officer. In 1974 he was given the additional title and responsibility of chairman.

The public knew Stalnaker as an untiring community activist and enthusiastic regional planner. He was chairman of the Regional Commerce

and Growth Association, a United Way campaign chairman, and a working member of Civic Progress. He was on the boards of Washington University, the Federal Reserve Bank, Barnes Hospital, the YMCA, Boys Scouts, St. Louis-San Francisco Railway, Brown Group, and Anheuser-Busch.

His associates knew him as a world-recognized industry pacesetter and spokesman and as chairman of the American Council of Life Insurance Companies, the nation's number one man in his own specialty. To those closest to him, he was husband and father and brother, family man, churchman, clubman, avid reader, holiday and weekend sailor.

Armand Stalnaker looked at St. Louis through a wide-angle lens and a long-distance telescope, and the view held a special beauty. To him, St. Louis was not just a grid of lovely or tawdry neighborhoods, but a community of human beings; a continuing drama of dreams and disappointments, of anger and frustration and loneliness, of pain and poverty and big and little triumphs.

"The organization which I think has the broadest perspective of any group open to me is the Regional Commerce and Growth Association," he said. "It isn't just downtown St. Louis. It isn't just Missouri. That appeals to me. Incidentally, it is almost unique among large city economic promotional organizations in that it includes both strong business involvement and strong labor representation, as well as educational institutions."

The former college professor, the mountain-bred boy with a Ph.D. in personnel psychology, delivered a textbook lesson in civic loyalty and pride, a loyalty and pride he expressed with fervor. But he was no Pollyanna in pinstripes. He was a tough-minded optimist with a practical streak who hoped for the best, trusted in life's essential goodness and the worth of every person.

"He's a blend of conservatism and adventure," said Dr. W. Edwin Magee, who often accompanied the Stalnakers on their forty-one-foot ketch from the Great Lakes to the coast of Maine to the Virgin Islands.

"He is an organized person who sets about things in a logical way and always studies the situation in advance to know exactly what he's going to do. Even when he could sail purely from visibility, within sight of land, he made a point of knowing where he was by compass.

"He knows what he can and what he can't do and how to stay out of serious trouble. That's the basic way he leads his life."

Stalnaker's career journey, while not unduly rough or uncertain, was a long one and followed a winding road. He was not born to the purple of corporate leadership. His heritage was of the hills, his bloodline that of a spirited people who saw more miners' caps than bankers' Homburgs, a people with too much heart and pride to believe they were poor.

"I read everything I could find in our little public library," he said. "By the time I started to high school, I knew I wanted to live in a different kind of town and a different kind of world."

When Stalnaker talked about his boyhood, he remembered especially the influence of two men. One was his grandfather, a thinker who loved to discuss ideas, despite his lack of formal education, a liberal interpreter of the Bible in a pocket of fundamentalism. The other was an Episcopal priest with whom young Armand spent many after-school hours discussing philosophy rather than dogma. Both helped shape and hone the boy's ethical convictions and religious faith.

That faith had no doctrinaire walls to shut people out. Admittedly disenchanted with rigid creeds of the more orthodox religions, he was attracted to the Society of Friends and its pacifism and nonviolence, beliefs which dominated his thought.

"The Quakers," he said, "have a fairly simple concept, which says, to use a Quaker phrase, 'There's that of God in every man.' This says something to me. It says something about capital punishment, about prisons, about mental hospitals, about war. It says something about 'the enemy.'

"These are God's people, you know, the Japanese and the Germans and the Russians. Whatever there is, of a kind of universal spirit, its best expression is probably that little spark that is in everybody."

Armand and Rachel Stalnaker were married in a Quaker meeting in Philadelphia. She was the daughter of Clarence Pickett, who for many years was secretary of the American Friends Service Committee.

"I have always been interested in people at work," Stalnaker said. "So my bachelor's degree was primarily in personnel, my master's from the University of Pennsylvania in labor economics, and my doctorate from Ohio State in personnel psychology.

"I thought I would teach all my life. I did teach at Ohio State and was in charge of the graduate placement office as well as developing research projects which business would fund, raising quite a bit of money for the school."

Even though he loved to teach and he and Rachel enjoyed working with students, he decided that if he were to be an administrator he'd rather be in a corporation than on campus. The business he chose was insurance, since he had sold policies during his vacations, and he joined the corporate office of Prudential, working first in personnel, then sales, training, market and psychological research and field office administration.

Thirteen years later, he was sought out by General American, and his first visit not only lured him from the New York area to the Midwest, but turned him into an instant St. Louis booster. Frederic M. Peirce, then president of General American, invited Stalnaker to meet members of the company board.

"What impressed me that day was that they were not only talking about General American, but also about St. Louis," Stalnaker remembered. "They all knew each other well. They were working together in the civic life of the community.

"I was also impressed by General American's remarkable history. It grew out of the failure of the old Missouri State Life Insurance Company and a corporate commitment to set up a new company which would honor all those policy obligations. It was one of the great stories of the insurance business."

For Stalnaker, that visit began an unabashed love affair with company and community. "The founders of this company built something out of a fiasco and built something for the policy holders. I think General American has occupied a position in this community which is prideworthy, although not unique."

When the company's old building at 15th and Locust streets began to buckle at the joints, the board had to decide whether to remodel or build and, if to build, whether in city or suburb.

"We wanted an identification with downtown St. Louis," said Stalnaker, "so I suggested that we put downtown the functions that should be there and put in the suburbs the functions that could best be done there."

Stalnaker's General American associates obviously were special people to him. "It is a great group," he said once. "Maybe we've been square as a company. We're not swingers. But we've been committed and dedicated and hard-working and proud of what we've done."

Stalnaker probably spent as many hours on civic work as on his company responsibilities, but neither was allowed to suffer. "He was an outstanding public servant, totally dedicated to the concept of corporate leadership being involved in civic affairs," said James O'Flynn, former president of the RCGA.

Stalnaker and Rachel, whose respective busy schedules often separated them, usually ended their days with a leisurely talk and walk around their neighborhood. Several times a year, but only for a week at a time, they put office and volunteer work on hold and took to the open waters.

Close as a family unit, they spent many vacations and special holidays with son Tim and his wife and son Tom and his wife. "Our home life means a great deal to both of us," said Stalnaker. "We have always lived fairly simply, in the Quaker tradition."

Stalnaker's thoughts turned to business. "There are two big questions which constitute both the opportunity and the cloud today," he said. "One, of course, is inflation. The other is where we are going to draw the line between social benefits provided to everybody through the tax mechanism and what responsibility individuals have for their own health and security.

"There's no way the government can give people everything they want as individuals. But the government can and should make sure they are never in real, critical need, never hungry, never cold, that their medical ills are treated.

"We could have a total economic collapse through overcentralization of government and benefits we don't pay for. But I would think the odds of my descendants living in a society that calls itself democratic and capitalist are rather better than a combination of all these things, such as bankruptcy and revolution."

Then, bringing his sights a little closer home, he looked at the future of St. Louis not as a city, but as a cooperative region. "I don't think that growth per se is a critical dimension," he said. "As a matter of fact, I think two million or so people is a great size. We are big enough to have cultural and sports and public events, and small enough to be a community. What I would like to see is improvement rather than growth."

Edward J. Schnuck

Deep in his heart, as with everyone, Edward J. Schnuck quietly harbored his special loves. His family. His friends. His work. His city. His country. But they were intertwined and inseparable, for here were his roots, his today, his tomorrow.

Schnuck was a shirtsleeved marketer in an informal and sociable workday world who was called "Ed" by the 5,400 members of his corporate family and whose office door was always open to anyone needing counsel or encouragement or help with a personal problem.

Schnuck moved gracefully from behind a counter to behind a desk, from the checkout cash register to the executive suite. From the first corner grocery store at Warne and Labadie avenues, the company expanded into supermarkets and into a corporation, reaching as far as Evansville, Indiana, and Fort Smith, Arkansas.

Ed Schnuck's life story was marked by surprise and paradox. As a boy, he scrambled for dimes and quarters with odd jobs in North St. Louis. In 1939 he and his parents opened their first store, although his father long had been a successful wholesale meat dealer. From his modest beginnings, he became a community activist, chairman of the Regional Commerce and Growth Association, vice-president of Civic Progress, general campaign chairman of the United Way, president of the St. Louis Council of Boy Scouts, director of the Backstoppers, Municipal Opera, Better Business Bureau, National Alliance of Businessmen, and Mayor's Economic Development Advisory Committee.

As a teenager, Ed left school to work, taking on more jobs at one time than many people handle in a lifetime. He later became a strong proponent of higher education as a trustee of Washington University, member of the Washington University Medical Center board of direc-

tors; on the president's council of Saint Louis University, and president of the board of Mary Institute. He was on the Barnes Hospital board of directors, on the lay advisory board of the Newman Foundation, and a member of the Washington University YMCA-YWCA campus branch; a director of the Multiple Sclerosis Society, Children's Home Society, and St. Louis Foundation for Alcoholism and Related Dependencies.

But as a boy growing up in hard-working, middle-class North St. Louis, Schnuck wasn't thinking much about the nuances of top-level business management and labor, or the area's economy. That was to come later.

Christened Edward James Schnuck in historic Friedens Church across the street from his birthplace at Nineteenth and Newhouse streets, he absorbed even as a little boy a sturdy Puritan ethic of independence and hard work. As the eldest of three children, he was earning money before he was out of knickers and into long pants.

When Schnuck was nine or ten, he held five different jobs at one time. He earned seventy-five cents a week burning trash and cleaning up for a druggist; delivered circulars for a butcher shop once a week; earned fifty cents for washing down the steps of a building from the third floor to the first; and on Saturday afternoons had a doughnut route. He delivered newspapers and had a newspaper stand at the corner of Twentieth and Salisbury streets, starting with the *Globe-Democrat* before dawn and ending with the *Post-Dispatch* long after dark.

When he was thirteen, lean and lanky and already tall, he became an apprentice bookbinder at George D. Barnard Printing Company, conveniently forgetting to bring his birth certificate every time the boss asked for it.

Edward's great-grandfather, Herman E. Schnuck, was a founder of Friedens Church, a strong anchor and religious mecca for the German families in North St. Louis. His grandfather, G. Edward Schnuck, was a powerful influence in molding his character and philosophy. His father was Edwin H. Schnuck, former owner of a wholesale meat company and founder, with Ed and his young son, Don, of Schnuck Markets. Edward's maternal grandfather was James Michael Donavan, from whom he inherited not only his Irish blood, but his second name.

The Schnuck penchant for work and fun, however, was passed along to the two sons and a daughter from both sides of the family. "Dad was a fun-loving, sweet and kind individual," Schnuck said of the pioneer meat merchant and food marketer who died in 1961. "He was a fantastic jazz piano player who had studied classical piano, but loved popular music."

Schnuck's Irish mother, who died in 1957, was a "strong power and a driving force," he remembered. She was also a talented pianist, and the children grew up with music as well as temperate discipline. From both parents came merchandising expertise, and he remembered particularly learning from his father "the business principles we follow today."

As a boy, Ed had spent fascinated hours watching planes take off and land at Lambert Field, and in his spare time he had learned to weld and to read blueprints at Robertson Aircraft. He had become the assistant purchasing agent at American Bakery Machine Company when he decided to join his father in the wholesale meat business, where he soon proved to have the energy of a steamroller and the soul of a Barnum.

"We bought an old truck for fifty dollars, repaired it, and with an attachment on Mom's vacuum cleaner painted it bright red with yellow wheels. It looked like a carnival truck," Schnuck recalled. "I got a school friend to paint a sign on the side—Schnuck's Wholesale Meats."

In 1939 came a turning point. "We learned that a little store at Shenandoah and Thurman avenues was closing and the chain owner wanted to sell the fixtures fast," Schnuck continued. "Dad decided to bid on them. We paid $250. I borrowed a hog truck from Grand Packing Company, got a half-dozen friends to help, and we went down on Saturday night and dismantled the store."

By coincidence, just at that time, his mother learned that the store at Warne and Labadie was vacant. "She and I went to look at it," said Schnuck. "The whole family, my brother and sister and I, pitched in to help. I installed the fixtures and built the shelving. We used one of the meat cases from the $250 purchase, and thirty days later we were in business."

It wasn't an easy life. "We would start work at four in the morning on the meat business and finish by noon; then I would go on to the store," he reminisced. "Dad would call our customers in the evening. The family took turns working in the store, but Mom really ran it."

As the store thrived, so did the family's dreams of expansion and growth, but those dreams would be postponed by World War II. Ed went to work at McDonnell Aircraft Company, starting as a riveter, then lead man, foreman, and finally, superintendent of the sub-assembly department.

After the war, Schnuck opened the first store on his own, a former Kroger store at Margaretta and Taylor streets. Meanwhile, his dad bought a former A & P Store at Manchester and Newstead avenues, and these became the nucleus of the present Schnuck Markets, Inc. Gradually, Ed, his dad, and his brother put together a family of seven stores, two of which were operated by Don. In 1952 came the giant step of consolidation and incorporation.

In 1970 they bought a local chain of twenty-five supermarkets, doubling, in one move, the size of their supermarket family. That same year, with the May Company, they launched the Venture supermarket-department stores. In 1976 the Schnucks formed a new company, entering into partnership with the Walgreen Company to operate Schnucks-Walgreen combination stores. Another area of growth was the Schnucks Station Restaurants located within some supermarkets.

The company's success, its chairman Ed Schnuck said from the corporate headquarters in Bridgeton, was built on a policy of friendly service as well as quality merchandise, with a dedication to integrity and honesty to employees and customers. "In our family and in our company," Ed emphasized, "we treat the other fellow as we want to be treated. It's not just a philosophy. It's a way of life."

The company has maintained a heavy schedule of employee activities throughout the year, in addition to giving special awards for outstanding service.

"Ed," his sister Annette Hanhardt said, "is a very humble man. He has the feeling that he is no better than anyone else, no matter how far he has come. He is a very loving man."

To talk to Ed Schnuck, even as to his siblings, Annette and Don, was to sense that their family ties were cords of steel wrapped in velvet. He brought into that long-enduring family circle his wife, the former Marilyn Gaddis. They have a daughter, Stephanie.

What are the good things about St. Louis as Ed Schnuck saw them?

"This is one of the leading medical centers in the country. It is probably safe to say it is the greatest. We have some of the finest universities in the country. There is a diversity of industry here. We have an excellent geographic location. There are more Fortune 500 headquarters here per capita than in any other city.

"We have retained the European work ethic. We have some of the best craftsmen, machinists, and metal workers in the country. Our quality of life is far above average. St. Louisans are fundamentally nice. There is less bigotry here than in most places of our country. Our renaissance, the rebirth of downtown St. Louis is a strong plus, as is a good highway system and good water—including our great natural resource, the Mississippi River.

"There's an above-average support of cultural activities. Our businessmen have the interests of the community at heart. It's one of the most efficient areas for the production of energy of all cities in the country. We not only have an ample supply, but the cost of energy in the 'sunbelt' is almost fifty percent higher. Also, we have a great natural gas supply.

"We have a positive labor-management image. The New Spirit of St. Louis Labor-Management Committee came about as the result of the example set by PRIDE, as well as an extremely negative report by a consulting firm. One idea is to create labor-management committees within companies and develop an exchange where either party can say something and not have it taken in an adversarial way."

"The great thing about St. Louisans—and Americans," he said, "is that they are so resilient. They can bounce back. I don't think we will destroy ourselves. I have great faith in the people."

Edward J. Schnuck died on February 5, 1987.

William H. Webster

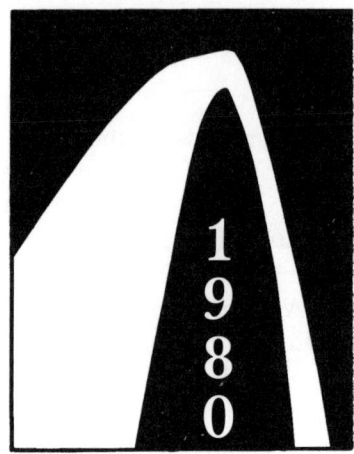

IT WAS THE MORNING AFTER the 1980 presidential election and in Washington, that Alice-in-Wonderland world of topsy-turvy dreams, the winds of change had ripped fading glories to tatters and dredged up gaudy hopes like dry leaves caught in the autumn breeze.

But at the city's heart, on a stone-enclosed island untouched by the swirling storm, the Federal Bureau of Investigation was moving with deliberate dispatch through another day of the government's war on crime and corruption.

The massive FBI complex didn't look like the battleground it was, set down in the middle of a city. The sun streamed into the courtyard as open and friendly as a city park, and hospitable signs welcomed tourists.

Even on the Bureau's off-limits floors there were no ghosts of cops and robbers, no lingering echo of the blood and thunder of colorful legend. Here instead in the nerve center where white collar crime and organized crime and public corruption became prime targets for FBI attack, the work went on in an aura of courtesy and quiet efficiency, a mirror of the character and modus operandi of the Bureau's number-one man.

William Hedgcock Webster, the straight arrow from St. Louis, placed his stamp indelibly on America's top crime-fighting agency, the FBI. Like Webster himself, the distinguished attorney and judge who moved from the security and prestige of the appellate bench into the middle of the capital's capricious maelstrom when he became FBI director in February 1978, the Bureau was a combination of spit-and-polish and old-shoe warmth.

Webster, a Republican, told reporters in 1980 that he had no plans

to pack his bags and had received no indication that he would not be retained by the Reagan administration. But as frequently as his extraordinarily crowded schedule permitted, he packed his bags to return to home soil in St. Louis, not only to visit with old friends, but also to fulfill his continuing role as a community leader.

The FBI chief graduated from Washington University School of Law, and his legal career began with a St. Louis firm. This led him to the mountaintop eminence of the Eighth U.S. Circuit Court of Appeals bench. He received honorary degrees from Washington University, as well as from Amherst, his undergraduate alma mater, DePauw University, William Woods and Drury colleges. He received a Washington University alumni citation for contributions to the field of law and the Distinguished Alumnus Award from the Law School. He was an active member of the Washington University board of trustees.

"I am convinced," he once told a Missouri crime prevention audience, "that the American people consider public corruption to be one of the most serious kinds of affronts. We have the obligation not to back away from this rather difficult and sometimes unpleasant undertaking. Our success in this effort will demonstrate that the law applies to the high and mighty as well as to the low and poor."

This focus, he said, "seeks to go beyond the streets into the upper echelon of crime," such as crackdowns on kickbacks in the shipping industry on the East Coast and pornography headquartered in the Miami area.

But the Webster imprint on the FBI was not that of a superpoliceman. Webster instigated and helped write a new FBI charter that was "an affirmative action of our mission and not just a series of 'thou shalt nots.' "

Webster grew up with that kind of respect for discipline and for the law. He was an only child in a close, affectionate family, but, as one friend recalled, he walked the long distance from his home on Yorkshire in Webster Groves to high school, because his father—who would pass him in his drive to work when Bill was halfway there—considered it good for the boy.

His mother died in 1967. His father, Thomas M. Webster, died in 1975, and Webster, then on the appellate bench, read his funeral service. "It must have been terribly hard for him," said a friend, "but that's the kind of person Bill is."

His dad, Webster said, was a disciplinarian, but not a harsh one. "It made us respect him, but we weren't afraid of him. He was always very patient. Because he was a jurist, he would always listen to the other side of the story."

Usually Webster was at his FBI office by 8:15 or so every morning, unless he had an early tennis game, which delayed the start of his work day about fifteen minutes. He frequently didn't leave until seven at night, after nearly all the staff had gone. His daughter, Katy, said of his tennis, "He has a good steady forehand and is a killer at net," and Bill, Jr., admitted he had been trying for a long time—without success—to beat him.

When the children were small, Bill, Jr., remembered, it was a house rule that everyone be dressed in time to have breakfast together. "We would talk about something in the paper that morning or something the family was concerned about."

His regard for impartial judgment led Webster to a study of Abraham Lincoln and particularly to the "compassion task" that Lincoln faced after the Civil War. "I don't profess to be a Lincoln scholar," Webster said, "but like any other boy growing up in the Midwest, I associated readily with him, and I have followed his writing and have studied the works about him.

"When I spoke to the Abraham Lincoln Association in Springfield, Illinois, we did a lot of research to contrast the assassination of Lincoln with the modern-day investigations, and it pointed up one of the recurring themes in my talks, that is, how you balance an increasing demand for privacy with the important job of collectively keeping society safe."

The balance between law enforcement and the protection of civil liberties permeated his FBI leadership, just as it did his judicial decisions. "He is the most fair-minded man I ever met," said Ethan A. H. Shepley, former vice-chairman of the board of Boatmen's National Bank. "His integrity is awesome. We got to know each other in law school. He has a sense of humor, but he was deadly serious about his work. I have never met anyone who so automatically gained the respect of everyone he met."

Shepley's words were echoed by other business and civic leaders. "He is super," said Dr. William H. Danforth. "I can't imagine anyone with a better balance between law and individual freedom. He agreed to take the chairmanship of the task force on the law school, even though he lived away from St. Louis. He wanted to maintain his ties with the university."

Webster's interest in Washington University was more than old school loyalty. "It is one of the three great universities which have meant so much to the enrichment of St. Louis," he said. "Washington, Saint Louis University, and the University of Missouri have helped make St. Louis great. But it is a two-way street. St. Louis, as a community, has given much to those schools and to the many other fine educational institutions of the community.

"When something needs to be done, St. Louis has never been a wasteland without leadership. We have always had people willing to take on heavy responsibilities, whether it's cleaning up the legal system or trying to put an anchor on poverty or decay or building a firm base for community giving.

"St. Louis has vitality and character. It has preserved its traditions but is open to new ideas and to progress. Many cities similar to St. Louis, with economic and population problems," he continued, "have experienced some long, hot summers, but the people of St. Louis and the leadership of the community have kept conversations going and have avoided disasters.

"I have confidence in the young people of today and in the quality of their education. Young people today are really not disillusioned. They are part of the solution. When we don't improve from one generation to the next, that is when we need to worry. Our institutions of government have held up under enormous pressures, and while we have been disillusioned from time to time about some particular branch of the government, still we don't take to the streets, but look instead to elective process and the courts and other kinds of solutions.

"It's a more complicated world we will face in the future, and we will still have to make some hard choices about what is important and where we want to put our resources, because they are finite. I would want my children never to lose their confidence in the world around them."

Zane E. Barnes

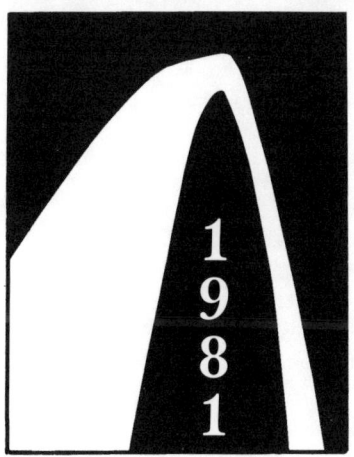

IT WAS WARTIME. Somewhere in the sunbathed vastness of the Gulf of Mexico, a ship wandered so far off course on its way from Galveston, Texas, to Jacksonville, Florida, that no landmarks could be sighted. On the bridge the young ensign, a neophyte navigator, was trying to chart the floating nomad's path. But without the nighttime stars, he had no way to reckon its position.

Scrambling some twenty-five feet to the top of the radar tower, he swept the endless waters with his binoculars. Suddenly he became aware of a tiny, rhythmic flash in the sky—the gleam from a light house on shore. He had found the answer to his problem.

Zane Barnes, that innovative ensign-navigator, later climbed skyward and has solved many problems since then. "There's usually an answer," he said. "It may take unconventional, creative thinking, but almost every problem can be solved."

The radar tower of those World War II days gave way long ago to a telephone pole and, in turn, to the corporate ladder. Barnes moved up from telephone lineman to field engineer to wire chief to vice-president to the prestigious post as president and chief executive officer of Southwestern Bell Telephone Company.

Zane Edison Barnes, corporate executive and community leader, didn't bury his modest beginnings beneath the patina of a comfortable lifestyle. The man who guided the destinies of a multi-million-dollar corporation never forgot that once he washed dishes for twenty cents an hour, or that he began his company career on a lowly level.

The urbane businessman, the disciplined telephone tycoon who structured his business hours with the precision of his cable-stringing days, remained an unpretentious man who loved to swim, golf, and play ten-

nis and whose hobbies ranged from wine connoisseur to bird watcher. No matter how hectic the day's schedule, or how late the meeting the night before, he got up early to enjoy a leisurely breakfast and watch the birds feeding outside his window.

Barnes came to St. Louis in 1973, and it was a mutual love affair from the start. He carved out time from his demanding schedule for a long list of out-of-the-office activities. He served on the board of directors of Alton Packaging Corporation, Burlington Northern, Inc., First National Bank in St. Louis, First Union Bancorporation, General American Life Insurance Company, and Interco.

His record of community involvements included the Arts and Education Council, Saint Louis Symphony Orchestra, Barnes Hospital, Jobs for Missouri Graduates, Jefferson National Expansion Memorial Association, and Missouri Public Expenditure Survey. He was a member of Civic Progress; was the 1977 campaign chairman and the 1978 president of the United Way; the 1977-79 president of the north central region of Boy Scouts; and the 1980 chairman of the "Pacesetters for Red Cross Blood Drive" campaign.

He was awarded the Silver Antelope for his contributions to the Boy Scouts and received the Americanism award of the Anti-Defamation League of B'nai B'rith. Barnes became a life associate trustee of his alma mater, Marietta College, and a trustee of Washington University.

"I really don't see how Zane gets so much done," said Dr. William H. Danforth. "He's a most effective executive, but he is always calm. I've never seen him when he looked harried or in a hurry. He arrives with notebook and pencil, prepared to do the job. He is a man of great good will."

The demanding schedule which took Barnes to his downtown office by eight every morning permitted few relaxing evenings at home and, at times, bordered on the mind-boggling. But the dual burden of corporate and civic leadership left no tell-tale trace.

Once, after a competitive tennis hour, Barnes determined to quit smoking. "I was playing tennis with an older man, and I noticed how much more energy he had. I also knew that he didn't smoke, so right then, I threw away the rest of my pack and haven't smoked since."

Barnes' early life in his native Marietta, Ohio, was no plush-lined existence. Divorce and death battered his family circle, and he and his younger sister, Dorothy, were reared by a cherished grandmother, "an ardent Baptist," he recalled, "a fine woman who loved her home and her roses and always encouraged us to do our best."

For young Zane, it was a good heritage. In his youth he "knocked around" on several jobs—in a restaurant, where he washed dishes, cleaned up and mopped the floor for twenty cents an hour, and in a laundry, where he didn't earn much more. When a friend gave him news about a possible job with the telephone company, his career road took a sharp turn.

"His father was wire chief for Ohio Bell, and my friend said they were hiring at the company," Barnes reminisced. "So, in 1941 I started as an installer-repairman, working in the plant department."

Once, he was climbing a telephone pole wearing heavy equipment, when a pack of snarling dogs surrounded the pole and stared up at him. He took off his belt and slung it around, but the dogs stayed and snarled. Finally, two little girls, about six years old, came by, and one of them picked up a stick and hit a dog over the nose. The whole pack ran away.

Barnes came down and asked the girl, "Did one of those dogs belong to you?"

"No," she said, "I just don't like mean dogs."

It was not a glamorous beginning, but Barnes believed he was "fortunate in that it gave me insight into the operations of the business which would have been difficult to obtain otherwise.

"I'm not sure that kind of beginning is necessary today," he continued, "because the nature of the business has changed so much. Basically today, we bring people in and give them a chance at managing, test them with actual experience."

But any such high position was far from young Zane's mind when, at twenty, his life took another unexpected turn. His grandmother died and at the same time an uncle became director of admissions at Marietta College. He and his wife—Barnes' mother's sister—became a second surrogate family for Zane and Dorothy.

Under the uncle's guidance, Barnes entered Marietta College, and after naval service during World War II, returned to gain his bachelor of science degree in liberal arts. "I was on the basketball team for awhile," he said, "but I found it was taking too much time. I had to work very hard in college because I hadn't been looking at books for a long time."

The young veteran's job at Ohio Bell had been guaranteed, but he decided to look around and was interviewed by several oil companies. "I wanted to go into a big business," he said, "where I could really get into operations in a hands-on environment. I wanted to go out into the oil field and learn how things were done."

When he was offered only sales jobs, he made another major decision. He went back to the telephone company. "I used to think that someday I would be a division manager," he said with a smile. "But I didn't dwell on that. I always had plenty at hand to occupy my mind. I really had no burning ambition to go up the ladder."

But that ladder was even then being put in place for the young man. In his four decades with the company, he saw changes as dramatic as the difference in the six phones he had in his home, from an old-fashioned pay phone to a sleek and sophisticated modern instrument.

A blend of pragmatist and dreamer, Barnes looked ahead to picture phones, electronic buying, fund transfers via telephone, and home security devices which "will alter the way we live."

"We do not expect to have all the market," he continued. "It will be a competitive market. The entire telecommunications universe will be expanded greatly and, therefore, no one should have a dominant share."

As Barnes continued to look ahead, he revealed an innate kindness and concern for the customer along with hard-nosed marketing expertise and a realistic look at the commercial world.

"We want to make it as easy as possible for the user," he said. "Unfortunately, there will be changes in pricing, an increasing rate for local services. But I feel that telephone service will remain a relative bargain among the necessities of everyday life.

"Our system of capitalism and free enterprise, put in historical perspective, can be held up as the highest standard of living in human history, and I don't mean by that just the things that people have. America, indeed, is the greatest country in the world. It is a place where freedom of expression, freedom for the individual, and freedom to live as one chooses are more available than anywhere else.

"This has been brought about by encouragement of the individual to take risks in the business environment and by being rewarded for taking risks, and not being dominated by central government.

"We all have to make sacrifices," he warned, "and to some extent the business and industrial community has to recognize that as programs previously funded by federal government are reduced, local initiative has to take up the slack. But the bottom line is that the individual must stand on his own feet."

What about the whole human society? Is he as upbeat?

"I'm not sure that we have made any significant strides in man's tolerance of man to the same degree that we have made technological strides," he said. "While most people today abhor the idea of men fighting lions in the Coliseum, we tend to be somewhat more tolerant of the 40,000 to 50,000 people killed in automobile accidents every year.

That may not be a fair comparison, but we may not have made as much progress in understanding ourselves as in understanding technology."

Barnes' look at St. Louis took him down a more practical pathway. "The building boom bodes well for our future," he said. "But you have to look at the whole metropolitan area and see that it has a great deal of potential.

"I believe it would be great to merge the city and the county. I recognize this would be extremely difficult and probably would not happen in one fell swoop, but working cooperatively within the framework of county and city toward mutual solving of mutual problems, perhaps we will get it all back together again. I would like to be a part of the action to help bring that about.

"The vitality of the county," Barnes explained, "can nourish the city, but the city also can nourish the county. Each has much to give to the other."

Clarence C. Barksdale

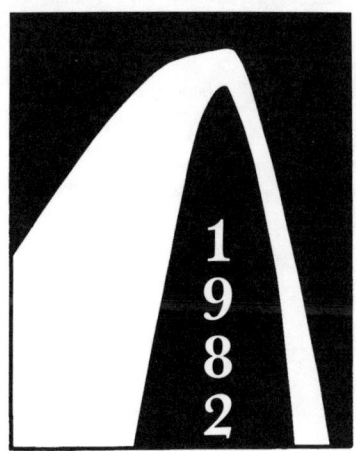

CLARENCE CAULFIELD BARKSDALE never fit the image of the stodgy tycoon in pin stripes. Rising in only twenty years from executive trainee to the prestigious posts of chairman and chief executive officer of Centerre Bank and Centerre Bancorporation, the lean and lanky Barksdale created his own special image as the new breed of money man, a skilled marketer, a pragmatic planner, more an administrator than a banker.

That was his candid self-appraisal. Others saw him also as a blend of small town sociability and big city sophistication, an aggressive community activist with the gusto of a whirlwind and the aplomb of an admiral, an urbane financier with an unabashed love for his river city in middle America. Despite his national recognition in the banking industry and his dominance as a St. Louis leader, he was as informal as the corner druggist and was known to employees, as well as to family and friends, by his nickname, Cedge, pronounced "Kedgie."

That holdover from boyhood surprised no one because Barksdale didn't really change a lot with the passing of the years. His father, the distinguished St. Louis lawyer, Clarence M. Barksdale, once told him that "too few people are willing to take charge, to take a risk." Cedge listened, learned, and marched into the fray.

For the one-time law student who switched to business because he wanted more action, his working days over the years became a blend of company and community commitments. He served on prestigious corporation boards, raised millions in charitable dollars, chaired school bond issues and the clean water drive. "I saw in banking," he said, "the same opportunities that originally drew me to law. Bankers had become the community leaders, and that's what I wanted."

A number of years ago, Barksdale was named to *Time Magazine's* list of those under forty-five considered likely to become national leaders, but his heart stayed in St. Louis. Said G. Duncan Bauman, former publisher of the *St. Louis Globe-Democrat*, "Cedge Barksdale's broad and active interest in our city has been a major stimulus in bringing about significant changes in the St. Louis community.

"Especially noteworthy is his service as president of Civic Progress. He was successful in changing the philosophy of Civic Progress from an organization which reacted to problems confronting it to an organization that pursues affirmative problem-solving before the fact."

" I have always aspired to the top job," Barksdale admitted with his native candor. "I was president of my class at Country Day School, president of my class at Brown University, president of my law school class at Washington University, of my fraternity." Cedge's friends said he probably could win another presidency—of the United States—if he really went for it. Politics was in his blood, inherited, along with his middle name, from his grandfather, former Missouri Governor Henry S. Caulfield.

"I always say the reason I aspired to the top at First National Bank was that the day I came to work here I saw William A. McDonnell arrive in a chauffeured limousine. I asked, 'Who is that man?' I was told he was the chairman of the board. I asked, 'Does someone always drive him to work?' That was the job I wanted."

Though he admitted he may have been motivated a bit by the fact that he hated to drive a car, still he climbed through increasingly responsible and prestigious jobs. In 1968 he became executive vice-president of Centerre Bank and in 1970 was named president—at thirty-seven, youngest in the institution's history. He became president and chief operating officer of the bank in 1973; president and chief executive officer of the bank in 1974; president and chief operating officer of Centerre Bancorporation in 1975; chairman of the board and chief executive officer of the bank in 1976, and chairman of the board and chief executive officer of Centerre Bancorporation in 1978.

"I had strong support from my family," he said. "My mother and father were always talking about the responsibility of leadership." When you are well-educated, they told him and his older brother, Henry, when you have "strength and good ideas, you also have a responsibility to take charge."

Pat Costello, his former secretary, said, "He is very much down to earth, an ordinary person. He is very concerned for the people. And he is a strong family man who makes a point of saving time for them."

"I was brought up with a great sense of family," said Barksdale. And that closeness has continued into the second generation. He called his mother nearly every day, and his wife, the former Emily Keyes— nicknamed "Nini"—has been her mother-in-law's good friend.

"I also had the blessing of wonderful grandparents we were very close to," Barksdale continued. "The governor and I would meet for lunch every week when I first came to the bank, just the two of us. My other grandfather was a druggist. He and grandmother were living in St. Louis when my father was born, but then moved to Sedalia and later to Branson. My dad went to school until he was sixteen, then he moved to St. Louis to live with relatives and finish school at Soldan. He was pretty much a self-made man. He went on to Washington University School of Law and that's where he met my mother.

"I have been blessed by having a really inspirational family life. There was a lot of discipline, but also a lot of love and support." That family closeness and pride were forged partly over bacon and eggs and pancakes. "My father always insisted we have breakfast together," Barksdale said. "He thought it was the best time in the day to communicate, even if that communication was silent, as it often was with teenagers. I continued that with my own two children.

"All my life, I had expected to become a lawyer like my father and grandfather," he said. "I had total respect for both. At Brown, I took courses which I felt would be a good general background for a legal career."

Then came the Korean action and Barksdale—obviously a man who wanted to control his own destiny—decided to choose his own branch of service rather than leave it to chance. And again his choice of the Army Counterintelligence Corps was a studied one, because he thought such investigative service would be helpful in law. And so, with a sense of adventure, the blithe young college graduate went to Berlin and entered the cloak-and-dagger world.

Out of the service with the rank of sergeant, Barksdale returned to St. Louis, entered Washington University School of Law and "dutifully prepared to follow my father and grandfather into the legal profession."

He had decided to forego the social life of the St. Louis debutante season in order to study and dug into the books with such determination that he was at his desk long after midnight. "Finally, Mother said, 'Cedge, you're getting dull. All you do is work.'

"She insisted I go to at least one party and it was there that I met Nini," he noted. "She was nineteen and I was twenty-five. I liked her right away. We saw each other at Christmas when she came home from Briarcliff and again during spring vacation."

They were married April 4, 1959, at her parents' home on Westmoreland Place. They are the parents of John and Emily, who was named for her mother and grandmother.

After a year in law school, Cedge told his father he just didn't like the law, and his father asked him to do one favor for him before giving it up, to spend the summer in his law office. Cedge was bored to death.

"Dad suggested I try the bank. They offered me $400 a month, which I turned down because I had another offer of $500. Then they said, $425, that's it. So I accepted and went through management training, starting on the first floor in new accounts."

From there Cedge Barksdale rose with the speed and flair of a meteor, and by 1968 he had become executive vice-president and was on his way to the top. After he assumed management of Centerre Bancorporation, the company chalked up significant growth. It became the largest bank holding company in Missouri, operating from sixty domestic locations and with international offices in London, Nassau, and Singapore.

What did he want for his city? What were its warts? Where was the beauty?

"We in St. Louis just need some additions to our infrastructure, and I have to assume there will continue to be a robust building environment," he said. "But we need to do a great deal more about the Port of St. Louis. That is vital to the success of our community. Then, of course, so is the relocation of the railroads, basically making this community more competitive in economic development.

"I guess my other dream at this point," Barksdale went on, "would be that someday the communities of the county and city would get together under one leadership."

What of America? What kind of world does he want for his children?

"Loving my country as much as I do," he said, "I still want us to have fifty or one hundred years from now the basic roots which have made us so great. As a businessman, I guess one of the most important is a free enterprise environment and a democracy which allows people to reach their dreams, but not a socialized society."

Scorning platitudes, Barksdale declared that while he recognized a need for America to be humane, "we need to take a serious look at our immigration laws. We have gotten *too* humane in this country. We are trying to do too much for too many people. We have to step back from some of these programs, reevaluate them and get rid of some. I wouldn't play God and say which we ought to give up.

"It's important for people to be able to stand on their own feet, and this is what I want for my children. My father always said, 'The only thing I can give you is a good education, and after that you are on your own.' I feel that very strongly."

As he walked to the window and looked out at the Gateway Arch and at his city and his river, he affirmed, "We have some great strengths in this country."

G. Duncan Bauman

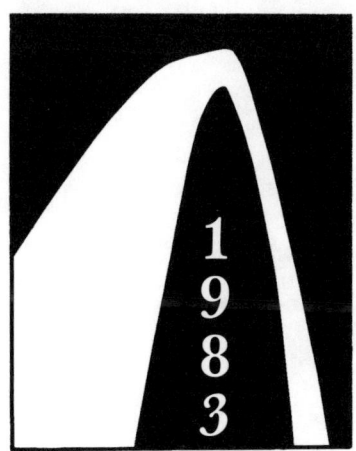

DUNCAN BAUMAN'S WORKING WORLD was the ordered quiet of the executive suite, but through the open door he heard the clatter of the city room. Much of his day was spent at board table or business meeting, at community or charity event, but his mind was never far from headlines and deadlines back at the office.

As publisher and editor of the *St. Louis Globe-Democrat*, he was a nationally known newspaper executive and a respected St. Louis mover and shaker and policy maker. He traveled the world and dined in the White House, walked with diplomats and talked with tycoons. Local observers called him one of the most powerful men in St. Louis.

In his journey from reporter's beat to corner office, from news cub to civic leader, a part of him stayed behind forever in the gaudy, Runyonesque world of *The Front Page*, that lusty, legendary age of American journalism now vanished in an era of computers and cold type. It was on William Randolph Hearst's *Chicago Herald-Examiner* that Bauman read his first byline and relished his first taste of journalism.

An attorney and a graduate of Washington University School of Law, he practiced before the Supreme Court of the United States, but the courtroom never held the magnetism of the city room.

To talk to him about his life, you sensed that George Duncan Bauman, community leader, was still "Dunc" Bauman, boy reporter. The saddest story he ever wrote was the obituary of his newspaper. He had announced in 1983 to his employees that the *St. Louis Globe-Democrat* was preparing to cease publication after 131 years. And Bauman, the newsman, grieved over its impending death.

"The best thing the *Globe-Democrat* did," he said "was to pursue a policy of presenting the news as impartially and fully as human beings

can produce it, consistent with the willingness of news sources to give the paper information."

With memberships or chairmanships in hosts of community, church and educational organizations, he was often at a meeting or special event four or five evenings a week and often on weekends.

A sampling of his activities: American Newspaper Publishers Association; executive board, Boy Scout Council of Greater St. Louis; former secretary, Board of Election Commissioners; former board member and president, Dismas House; state chairman, Missouri Committee for Employee Support of the Guard and Reserve; former board member and president, Child Center of Our Lady of Grace; national board, Junior Achievement; board member, Boys Club of America; DePaul Community Health Center lay advisory board; former president, Herbert Hoover Boys Club; vice-chairman, Missouri Baptist Hospital board of trustees; Policemen's and Firemen's Fund; former board member and president, Catholic Charities; trustee, David Ranken Jr. Technical Institute; President's Council, Saint Louis University.

His community involvement earned him more honors and citations than could be found in a Pentagon roomful of five-star generals. He was awarded three honorary doctorates, was a Knight of Malta, received a medal for distinguished public service from the U.S. Department of Defense, the Right Arm of St. Louis Award from the St. Louis Regional Commerce and Growth Association, the Silver Beaver Award from the Boy Scouts of America, and was elected to the Missouri Academy of Squires.

He was named Man of the Year by the Variety Club, Man of the Year by the St. Louis Police Relief Association, received the Conspicuous Service Medal, highest civilian honor of the Missouri National Guard.

"Dunc epitomizes the very best of St. Louis citizenship," said William H. Webster, former director of the Federal Bureau of Investigation. "He is a deeply caring person and doesn't hesitate to put himself on the line for the people and the community and the country he cares so much about."

Bauman, a fighter, came out swinging, whether he was outraged at some community or at an official or at labor or management or at individual malfeasance, or if he was stumping for support of a project to better the community and its people.

The one thing that made him really angry was to learn that someone had lied to him. "I absolutely detest liars," he declared with the vehemence usually reserved for a far-left liberal press. "They ought to be exterminated!"

A devout conservative, Bauman also took out after his own industry, especially those editors on the other side of the political- philosophical fence.

"I am optimistic about America's future," he said "because at the present time, except for the misrepresentation of the liberal press, the American people are very soundly behind a strong America and the perpetuation of the values of this country." A devout Catholic, he not only was honored by his own church, but received many awards from the Jewish community. The St. Louis Rabbinical College conferred on him an honorary doctor of humane letters degree in 1981, and he received the Silver Crown, the highest honor given to an individual. Bauman, the first non-Jewish recipient, was described as "a prisoner of truth . . . a man with a great sensitivity" who has demonstrated "a wonderful feeling for the disadvantaged."

Bauman's innate courtesy and standards of behavior, his social conscience, his political views and his religious faith were inherited from his parents—Peter W. Bauman, who came to America from Germany as a seven-year-old, and Mae Duncan Bauman, daughter of a farmer-merchant-banker of Humboldt, Iowa.

Early in Duncan's life, the family moved to Tulsa, Oklahoma, where his father built downtown commercial property and owned an interior decorating firm for some years until they moved back north to Chicago and on to Wilmette, a North Shore suburb. Their family life was a pleasing blend of parental love, strict adherence to religious and ethical standards and sometimes stern discipline. "I remember him as my big brother," said Gini Matthei. "He was always a very responsible child, an excellent student, and he was never in any trouble."

As a teenager, Bauman entered Loyola Academy, then went on to graduate from Loyola University. He was not only an excellent student but a track star. He was working part-time and going to law school at Loyola, but ultimately stopped school and started working full-time. It was at this time that he met and married Nora, as Irish as her surname, Kelly, who through the years became so enmeshed in her husband's career that she often spoke of the *Globe-Democrat* as "we" or "us" and frequently referred to Bauman as "the boss."

They had no children, but he was a godfather, and he and Nora welcomed his younger brother, Bill Bauman, as a guest in their home while he attended Washington University School of Law. When Bauman went to the *Globe-Democrat* in 1943 after a brief stay with another St. Louis firm, he took some *Front Page* flair with him, said Martin Duggan former editor of the editorial page and then-chief of the copy desk.

"He was night city editor and was on the desk on Sunday, always a slow day," said Duggan. "One day we got a tip that King Farouk of Egypt was interested in a young St. Louis woman, Mimi Medart, daughter of a St. Louis restaurateur, who later married the 11th Earl of Coventry. Dunc decided we should go right to the source, so he got one of the copy desk men who could speak French to put in a long distance call to Egypt and ask for a statement." All they ever got out of Farouk—when he finally understood the question—was "Mimi who?" But at least Dunc Bauman had his story.

From the city desk, Bauman went on to be personnel manager and business manager before he succeeded the late Richard H. Amberg as publisher and editor in 1967. As he advanced in his professional career, he became increasingly prominent on the St. Louis scene. And his love for his adopted city grew.

"The great thing about this community is exemplified in our Old Newsboys Day," he said. "People with the most wealth and the broadest resources and the people with least resources universally support community needs. We are one of the few cities in which, when it becomes necessary to solve a community problem, the key leadership gets out and does the work. It doesn't assign subordinates to get the job done."

If these are St. Louis' strengths, what are the city's faults?

"The one major problem St. Louis had for a long time—and it has largely dissipated—was the self-denigration." St. Louis, he added, could be proud of many things. "One, without question, is our civil rights record. The archbishop of St. Louis desegregated the Catholic schools in 1947, and almost immediately, the public schools began to follow suit.

"Then we came to the 1960s and 1970s and we didn't have the problems of a Watts or a Detroit or a Washington or a Chicago. That was due to the good will among the blacks and whites which developed slowly over the years. Also, our downtown development has been unbelievable."

But sharing his pride in civic achievements is his pride in heading a newspaper which had a major role in the community betterment. That's one reason. In fact, Bauman devoted his whole professional life to the newspaper business.

And, through the open door of his corner office, Duncan Bauman, the newsman, was always listening to the clatter from the city room.

Sanford N. McDonnell

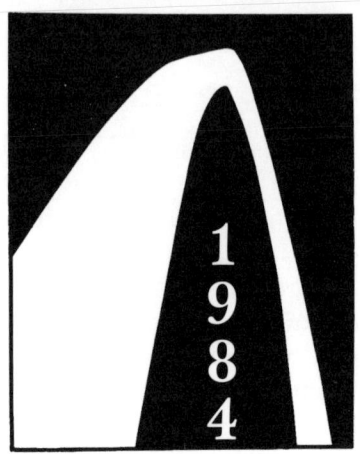

At Princeton, he studied economics. At the University of Colorado and Washington University and in the army, he studied engineering. His prestigious career was a blend of the two. On his way to the chairman's seventh-floor, glass-walled office, he learned about aerodynamics and how to design and manufacture aircraft. Economics and engineering became a natural partnership. Both were in his blood.

Although, as a boy growing up in Little Rock, Arkansas, he was famous in the family for saving his allowance and spending his funds wisely, he credited his father, banker William A. McDonnell, with instilling in him a respect for sound financial planning. And although, to his mother's dismay, he used to lead his friends in derring-do leaps from roof to tree to ground, he learned his special love of wings and of the skies from his uncle, James S. (Mr. Mac) McDonnell, a venturesome pioneer who founded the corporation out of his hip pocket.

But the lanky business and community leader, known up and down the personnel ladder as "Sandy," placed his own stamp on the corporation he headed, and the community which became his adopted home. Since 1939, when a rented office in a two-story brick building near Lambert International Airport became the incubator for an industrial complex, and James S. McDonnell and his secretary were the only employees, personnel increased to more than 86,000 in St. Louis; southern California; Tulsa; central Florida; and Toronto by 1984. It was by far Missouri's largest private employer.

Sandy's stewardship got much of the credit for company growth. Though the skies over the fiercely competitive aerospace market were not always friendly, Sanford McDonnell—commented the *Wall Street Journal* after evaluating his first year at the controls—passed his "early tests

with ease." Appropriately, for a young man entering the aerospace industry, he took flying lessons and got his instrument rating and twin-engine license. "I had about 1,100 hours, but I gave it up when I became president of the corporation, and also we got rid of our propeller planes," he said.

Like nearly every other corporate executive in America, he took a loaded briefcase home every night. However, before tackling the paperwork, he customarily relaxed with his wife and enjoyed an unhurried dinner. One hobby has been the piano. He often played in the evenings while his wife, Priscilla, sang. An accomplished musician, a graduate of Julliard, she formerly was the contralto soloist at Ladue Chapel and maintained a lively interest in St. Louis cultural activities, serving on the boards of the Saint Louis Symphony Society and the Arts and Education Council, among other community organizations.

"I had always been interested in drawing and sketching," McDonnell said. "I had studied art in college and even in the army, and I knew I would get back to it. But the years kept slipping away, so in 1978 I decided this was the time." A number of bronze figures on the grand piano and in a lighted wall cabinet reflected a talent in that art medium. His musical gifts, admittedly, were more modest. "As a pianist, I'm very mediocre," he said, "but I love it."

An elder at Ladue Chapel, he has been candid about his love for the Bible and his staunch religious faith. He often played hymns, interspersed with popular tunes and the classics. His wife and his associates at work agreed that McDonnell seldom raised his voice or was upset or angry. McDonnell's early religious training was in the Episcopal Sunday school in Little Rock, Arkansas, where he was born October 12, 1922, to William A. and Carolyn Cherry McDonnell. His sister, Cherry, was born two years later. "He was a serious little boy," said his mother of Sanford, "and a leader in the neighborhood. He was always responsible, but he was also venturesome. I remember watching him and his friends leap from the roof to a big tree. It would curdle the blood."

Sandy was a young adult when his parents moved to St. Louis in 1944. When he returned from naval service after World War II, his father was president of the First National Bank and a distinguished leader in the financial community. Sandy, as a former economics student, might have been expected to follow that career.

"He was always very frugal as a child," said his father. "He had an allowance, but never in his life did he ask for a nickel."

During the depression, at the time of the bank moratorium, the senior McDonnell did not want to take any money out of his bank—and Sandy was the only one in the family who had any cash. He still kids them about tiding the family over during those critical hours.

"I worked in the bank in Little Rock as a boy," Sandy said, "and for lack of anything else, when I went to Princeton, I thought I would take a business course. I worked in the Little Rock bank during the summers, but Dad didn't want to be a heavy influence on where I worked or what I would do. He gave me that independence.

"I got my bachelor of arts degree from Princeton in absentia because I was in the army. The army sent me to engineering school. That's when I became interested in engineering and later decided to get my degrees at the University of Colorado and Washington University." He spent two of his three years in the army on the atomic bomb program in Los Alamos, and that's where he met Priscilla Robb, who became his wife. They were expecting their first child, Robbin, when Sandy joined his uncle's company.

Two years later, their son, William Randall (Randy), who was to become the inspiration for his father's deep interest in the Boy Scouts, was born. On that October day in 1948, when Sandy was to report for work, Mr. Mac asked him to stop at his home for breakfast. "We talked about the job and he suggested that I might start at the lowest rate, janitorial work, at sixty-eight cents an hour, so that I could say as I went up the ladder that I had started at the bottom.

"I had been attending the University of Colorado on the GI Bill, getting $125 a month, and Pris was on the faculty at the university teaching voice in the music school and making $275. When I got to St. Louis, she was pregnant and no longer supporting me. I told Mr. Mac that I didn't think much of his idea, that I wanted to start at the going rate for someone with my education." His uncle obviously respected his spunky answer. He hired him as a trainee at $1.26 an hour.

In 1962 he was elected a director and became vice-president and general manager of all combat aircraft. The following year he was elected to the executive committee and in 1966 became president of McDonnell Aircraft Company. In 1967 he was elected director of McDonnell Douglas Corporation, created from the merger of McDonnell Aircraft and Douglas Aircraft. In 1971 he was elected president of the corporation and the next year chief executive officer. In 1980 he was elevated to chairman and chief executive officer and chairman of the McDonnell Douglas Foundation, formerly McDonnell Aerospace Foundation.

"Mr. Mac was a terrific guy to work for," Sandy said. "He was hard to work for, very tough. He demanded time and excellence out of everyone. It was not easy at times, but it was a tremendous experience."

Sandy continued to support United Nations Day, a paid holiday initiated in the firm by Mr. Mac, and in his office stood the Stars and Stripes of his own nation, along with accents of Scotland, the land of some of his ancestors. The company's founder used to refer to himself as "the old Scotsman," and Sandy inherited pride in the family's Highland blood.

He identified himself as "Sandy" in his announcements over the public address system and in his printed messages to the employees in the company newspaper, and he encouraged his associates to call him by his nickname. "I think it is terribly important that the people of America start reversing a trend of lack of trust of business, of the school systems, colleges and universities, the government, even the church. The only way we can turn that around is for everyone to start trying to live up to a code of ethics like the Scout Law or like our own code of ethics which we adopted at McDonnell Douglas in April 1983."

An ardent patriot with a dream for America, he often spoke at public meetings of that dream with candor.

"Greatness as multi-faceted as the greatness of the United States has, naturally, many different causes," he said. "Some of these causes are material, physical, measurable things. But the most important sources of our greatness are not tangible at all. They're spiritual, unfashionable as that word may seem today. And you measure them not in tons or square miles but in terms of the traditions passed down to us by Americans of past generations."

Charles F. Knight

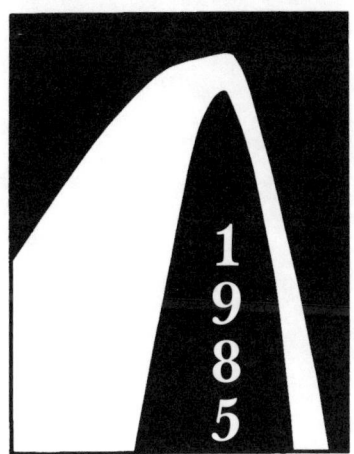

Whhen he was scooting up and down the gridiron as a first string end for Cornell University, Chuck Knight was making his mark as a young man in a hurry who knew where the goal line was. Programmed for success from childhood by his hard-driving father, Knight built his own career on an inherited formula:

"A sense of urgency, dedication to excellence, recognizing the challenge even when things are going well."

Along the way he learned to laugh at timetables for job advancement. He didn't suffer waiting gladly.

When he joined Emerson Electric in December 1972 as the hand-picked heir apparent to W. R. ("Buck") Persons, the agreement was that "if it worked, he would make me chief executive officer in three years. He did that in six months. In eighteen months, he made me chairman of the board," Knight said.

Knight spoke of his jet-propelled climb without ego or apology. This was a man, his associates said, who respected himself and his abilities and dealt in facts, not fantasy.

At Emerson, he fit the mold as though it had been designed just for him. Then he added his own stamp and personality. Knight's record did not go unnoticed. In 1981 he was cited by the heads of *Fortune's* 500 as one of America's five best CEO's, and Emerson was rated as one of the nation's four best-managed corporations. *Time Magazine* listed him among the "50 Faces of the Future."

In 1976, only three years after his arrival in St. Louis, Knight received the St. Louis Award. At the ceremony, then-Mayor John Poelker said of the transplanted Chicagoan, "We are privileged that from time to time someone comes in from the outside and challenges us."

Born in Lake Forest, Illinois, and reared on Chicago's North Shore, Knight moved with ease from the shores of Lake Michigan in 1972 to the banks of the Mississippi. He became an instant St. Louis loyalist. Although his personal and professional world centered in home and the executive suite, that world encompassed the whole metropolitan area and a long list of special projects.

By his choice, most have been in St. Louis. Among his many civic affiliations: trustee of Washington and Cornell universities; member of the executive board of the St. Louis Area Boy Scout Council; director of Barnes Hospital, Missouri Botanical Gardens, Olin Foundation, Arts and Education Council; chairman of Civic Progress, University of Missouri, United Way, *Globe-Democrat* Old Newsboys Day, and Mathews-Dickey Boys' Club.

"You have to make the decision," Knight said, "whether you can dedicate your time on a national basis or whether you want to give that time to the community. I'm not saying you can't do both, but you have to decide where to put the focus. I made the decision that I want to devote that time to St. Louis. You can be more effective at the local level."

When he was elected president of Civic Progress—prior to becoming chairman—he changed the traditional afternoon meetings and follow-up cocktails to breakfast sessions. He wanted to save everyone's time.

When Chuck was fourteen, his father, who headed an engineering management firm, sent him on the first of his summer assignments to work in factories and offices all over the world. This wasn't fun and games. This was Lester Knight's way of giving his son a boost, of making sure the boy had first-hand experience in the massive, complex world of business and finance. Chuck did a lot of dirty jobs .

Lester Knight's training regimen paid off. As Chuck said, "I could never have done the job without the training he gave me and the experience of owning a business and having to meet the payroll. I got that from a very young age and I will be forever indebted to the man for his interest in me."

And despite the hard work, it was a pleasant, comfortable childhood for Chuck and his only sister, Leslie, later Mrs. Robert Abbott, Jr., of Weston, Mass. "Mother was the glue in our family," he said. "Dad was a hard-working, hard-charging, very successful businessman who taught me that you have to get your priorities straight in life."

As much as Chuck admired his dad, he did have a will of his own. While still at Cornell, he wanted to marry Joanne Parrish, daughter of *Chicago Tribune* cartoonist Joseph Parrish and Chuck's childhood sweetheart. His father insisted he wait until after graduation.

Chuck wouldn't wait. He married anyway and to support his new bride he coached freshman football at Cornell, taught plumbing at the hotel school and graphics at the engineering school. He completed his formal education, receiving his bachelor's degree in mechanical engineering and his master's in business administration.

Then he was sent abroad as a management trainee with a major German piston ring manufacturer. Here he not only learned the business, but became fluent in German.

Now the apprenticeship was over. Chuck was ready. His first assignment was as head of Lester B. Knight International Corp., a subsidiary of the Chicago-based parent firm. In three years, he built its international volume from one million dollars to more than five million annually. His future, it appeared, was set.

But one day in 1963, while Chuck was still abroad, he received a cable from his father which was to change that future dramatically and, in time, have a major impact on the future of St. Louis: "Be in St. Louis Monday morning," read the cable, "or you're off the payroll."

His new assignment was to serve as a management consultant for Emerson Electric. Emerson and Buck Persons had been Lester Knight's clients for nearly ten years, and now those clients were Chuck's responsibility. Knight did the job so well that when Persons was ready to choose his successor, he didn't have far to look. Chuck was his choice.

At Emerson Knight surrounded himself with capable team members and expected them to deliver. But he also gave them a lot of free rein. He didn't mind their standing up to him—he welcomed their ideas—but they'd better do their homework and be ready to argue him down.

Chuck Knight has worked as hard as any man, harder than most. He was frequently at his office by 6:30 or 7:00 A.M. and not at home again for twelve hours. Joanne long ago learned not to worry about serving dinner at a set time and hasn't let herself get upset about last-minute business appointments or cancellations.

"But he's pretty good about keeping dates," she said. "When he commits himself, he will do it."

Knight has made sure there was time for fun with the close-knit family in spite of his schedule. The family usually is together for holiday dinners and other special events and for vacations in the Michigan home built by his great-grandfather. He has taken his four children on his favorite adventures, African safaris. Even though his family and his career have been at the core of his life, Knight found it hard to say no to the tremendous tugs on his time to the community.

Ten years ago, when the St. Louis public schools were threatened with loss of their athletic programs because of a lack of funds, Knight organized a fund drive, "Save Our Sports," which raised $250,000 and brought him the St. Louis Award. Under his leadership, Civic Progress backed a sales tax increase to generate funds to promote economic development in the community and build the status of economic development activities within the state government.

"Thinking of what has been accomplished in the past ten years," he said, "I feel we now have a tremendous momentum. If we can avoid fractionalization between city and county and keep the cooperation and get the help of the governor where we need state help in maintaining our infrastructure, I think we will attract industry and avoid a job drain.

"The big issue here, the big challenge, is economic development. It's not politically feasible to merge the city and county, but we should be looking at ways to cooperate. The regional hospital is a wonderful example of that."

Knight's love of St. Louis has been a microcosm of his love of America. "I have seen so many good things happen because one person, or just a few people, have believed that they could happen and have worked to make them happen. One person working alone, with a clear idea of what needs to be done, can often change the course of mighty institutions for the better, for the common good."

Lee M. Liberman

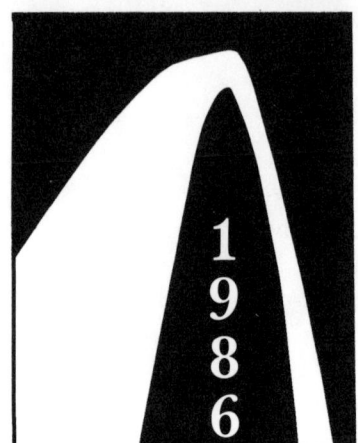

FROM HIS SPACIOUS OFFICE on the fifteenth floor of the Laclede Gas Company building, Lee M. Liberman looked out at the river, the Arch and the malls, at the silhouettes of new buildings standing tall against the downtown sky, and at landmarks grown worn and familiar with the passing of the years. He listened to the city's heartbeat and the muted rhythm of the traffic far below.

This was his city and his world.

It was here, on an autumn day in 1945, that he walked through these downtown blocks and, in what seemed at the moment a random decision, changed the course of his life.

If he had just walked a little farther that day, he might have been selling electricity instead of natural gas. Or if he hadn't been looking for a temporary job instead of just "fiddling around" before going back to school, he might have become a lawyer instead of Laclede's chief executive officer.

Discharged from the air force, he returned to St. Louis to relax before entering Stanford University Law School. He had graduated from Yale University with a degree in chemical engineering, then had gone into active service and was training to be a bombardier when the war ended.

"I thought I would take it easy for awhile, but none of my friends was out of service yet, and all the girls I knew were married," he said. "I did nothing for about nine days and thought I would take a job until January.

"I went to the employment service, and they sent me on two job interviews, one at Laclede and one at Union Electric. Laclede was closer, so I stopped there first. I didn't tell them I didn't mean to stay long." Certainly he didn't plan to stay the rest of his working life. But when

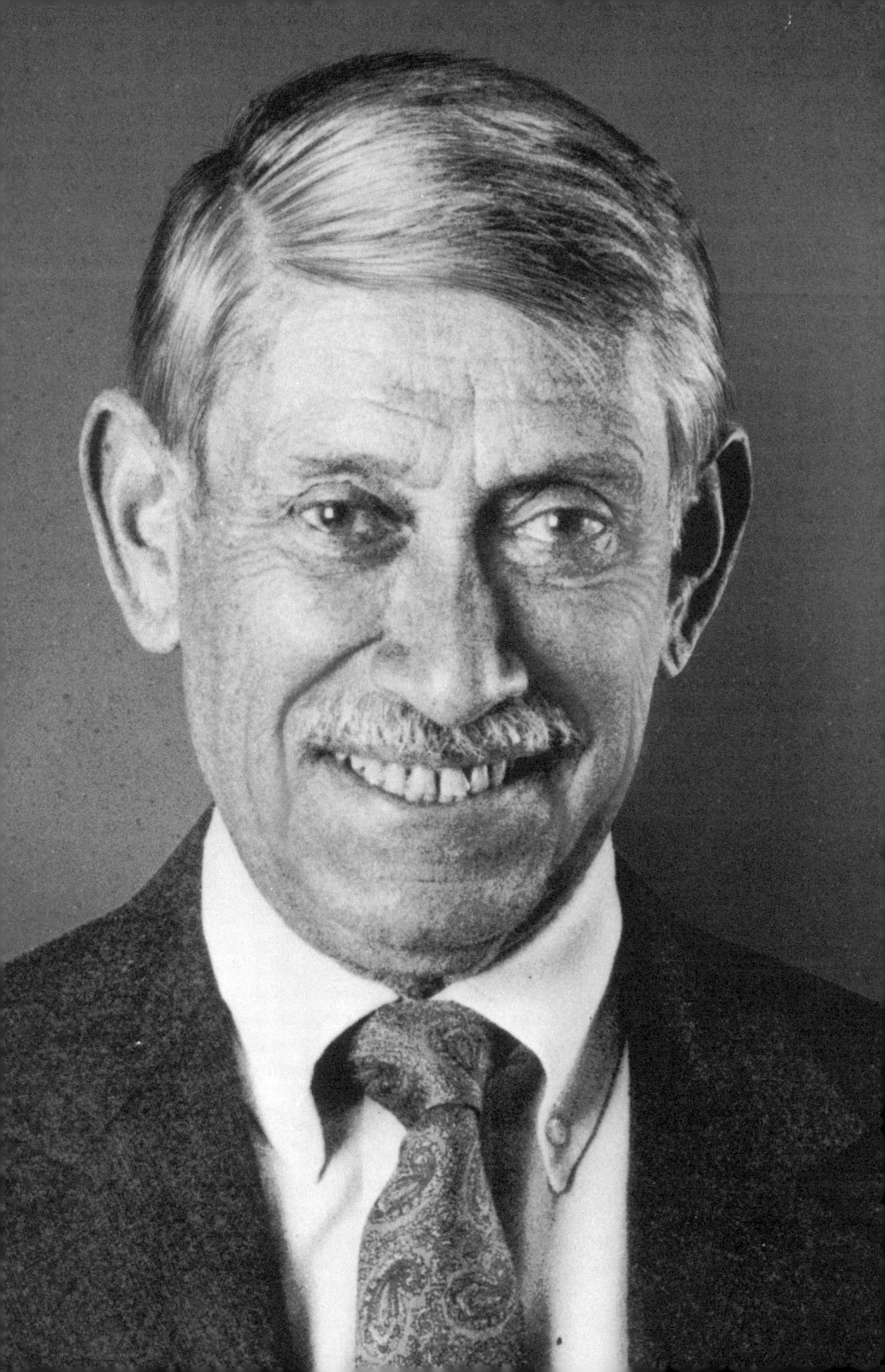

he was offered his first job at Laclede's coke plant on South Broadway, the die was cast.

"Laclede didn't have a job for a chemical engineer, but they did hire me as a chemist. My clothes smelled so much like gas that when I got home, everyone thought there was a gas leak in the house."

Of such coincidences is shaped many human pilgrimages. But regardless of the direction Liberman's own pilgrimage ultimately took, he still would have become a civic activist and community leader. That's the Liberman lifestyle. "I just think it's important to give something back," he said.

Lee Liberman would not be chosen from central casting as the image of a captain of industry. An unassuming man, his conversation was low-key, and he apologized when the conversation turned inward and he talked about himself. Yet he was a mover and shaker, a quiet battler, a man of influence who became president and chief operating officer of his company in 1970; chief executive officer in 1974; and chairman in 1976.

As he climbed the corporate ladder at Laclede and involved himself in the community, he gave much to St. Louis. In that time span, his business and civic activities reached an extraordinary range—from the board room of the affluent to the sick room of the indigent; from the executive suite to education, symphony to Scouting, culture to charity, art to health care.

Liberman was chairman of the Regional Commerce and Growth Association and vice chairman of Civic Progress. He has been president of the Executive Service Corps of St. Louis, chairman of the Salvation Army Tree of Lights, and chairman of the United Way campaign. He was chairman of the 1985 NAACP annual dinner; president of Family and Children's Service and the Backstoppers; chairman and trustee of Jewish Hospital; a trustee of Washington University and Washington University Medical Center; trustee or director of Cardinal Glennon Hospital and the Arts and Education Council.

"He is a man of boundless energy with a great desire to help his fellow man," said Edwin S. Jones, former chairman of the board of the First National Bank in St. Louis. "He is a remarkably friendly person who has gained the admiration of everyone he has known."

"Lee is a man of great compassion," added G. Duncan Bauman, retired publisher of the *St. Louis Globe-Democrat*. "He is warm-hearted and concerned, but he is always a fighter for what he believes is right. He is recognized as a tenacious person determined to achieve an objective once a goal has been selected and always with forthright candor."

The familiar Liberman chuckle broke through the conversation as he recalled his first contacts with corporate and civic leaders when he was a young Laclede executive.

"I remember when I was thirty years old and we were in the old building. Bob Otto [Robert Otto, then chairman of Laclede] would hand me a stack of pledge cards and send me out to solicit financial support for some community projects. I was so nervous that I would have to walk around the block three times before I could get up the courage to talk to those men. I still don't like to collect money."

Lee's father, Ben Liberman, was a distinguished St. Louis lawyer and member of the board of police commissioners. His uncle, Sam Liberman, was also a lawyer and a police commissioner, city counselor, and president of the St. Louis Bar Association. Lee's older brother, James, followed the family pattern of law and became a corporate attorney in New York.

The family moved to St. Louis from Salt Lake City, where Lee was born on July 12, 1921. They settled in the Central West End, and Lee graduated from Soldan High School. Even in their young years, Liberman recalled, he and James, five years his senior, had lively discussions with their parents about public service and the nation and politics.

"My parents were both brilliant," he said. "Our household was pretty vibrant and exciting. Of course, we were living in a vibrant and exciting age."

If Lee had a hero, it was his father. "He was an intellectual, a man for all seasons," Liberman said. "There was nothing going on that he didn't know about, whether it was history or current events or translating my Latin or my son's Latin or my grandson's Latin. He could even translate it over the telephone.

"It was a happy household. I never heard him raise his voice. He always talked in calm, measured tones. He had an amazing breadth of knowledge. Unfortunately, I didn't inherit all of that, but I was the beneficiary."

But he and his dad weren't spending all their time discussing presidential elections and current events. After the family moved to St. Louis, Ben and Lee became ardent Cardinal baseball fans and spent many Sunday afternoons at double-headers at old Sportsman's Park.

It was in those days, too, that Scouting became so much a part of his life. In 1938 Lee attained the high status of Eagle Scout. As an adult, he served on the local council, executive board, and advisory council. Among his most treasured mementos was a handsome plaque presented to him by the National Court of Honor through the St. Louis Area Council to commemorate his more than a quarter-century of Scouting activity as a youth and adult and awarding him the high honor of Distinguished Eagle Scout because "he has continued to serve his God, his country, and his fellowmen, following the principles of the Scout Oath and Law."

By marrying the former Ann Medler, Liberman acquired two stepsons, Peter and Andrew. By an earlier marriage, he was the father of Alise O' Brien, a photographer; Celia Hosler, a partner in an underwriting company; and James Liberman, a Chicago architect.

Ann Liberman carved her own niche in the community life of St. Louis as an active volunteer, with special emphasis on education and art.

Liberman did not claim to be a classical music scholar, although he took piano lessons as a child and became a good listener of the classics when he was in college. But his leadership of the Saint Louis Symphony Society was one of his most satisfying community activities. He saw the symphony and other cultural entities not only as tasty icing on the civic cake, but as essential elements of community life.

"It's hard to put your finger on what is so good about St. Louis," he said, "because it is so unusual and such a great place to live. We have everything here that even larger cities have—good symphony music and good opera, the art museum, Shaw's Garden, all great cultural things. We have great educational institutions and sports."

As a corporate executive, Liberman equated such advantages with a healthy civic economy. "I think the quality of life here is the most important selling point of our area. There must be something to it. People don't want to leave. We have talked with some who probably thought they were coming to a cultural wasteland. But they don't want to go back to New York or the other cities where they came from. The more jobs we have, the more people who come in, the better we can maintain our community and its culture."

Creation of jobs through new industry was a major concern of Liberman and the Regional Commerce and Growth Association. "We have had a pretty ambitious program," he said. "We have to retain jobs and create new ones. We have service and fast food jobs, but those are low paying. We need more technology."

"Health care for those without means to pay is a very serious problem. I hate to see a society where people who can afford it live long lives and those who can't afford it are disregarded. It is one of our greatest problems, but it is difficult to make progress."

On the subject of the federal government, he considered the deficit the nation's major problem. "If you had asked me years ago," he said, "I would have told you that inflation was our greatest problem. But now it is the deficit. It is great that we were able to conquer inflation, but we haven't been able to conquer the deficit.

"We either have to raise taxes or cut back on social programs, and that is difficult to do. Obviously, there is a lot of waste in social programs, but I do think society has a responsibility for the less fortunate."

As a corporate leader, Liberman did not agree that America could maintain itself as a great nation by becoming a service economy. "I think we have got to manufacture goods and have some basic industries. My major concern is that our basic industries are not well. We have exported a lot of our manufacturing to places like Japan and Korea. People say we import a lot of goods. I like to look at it the other way—that we export a lot of jobs."

But the country is not "going down the tube" despite its troubles, he insisted. Although there are problems, the future isn't bleak in Liberman's eyes. From his office window, looking at the river and the Arch, the old buildings and the new, listening to the sounds of the traffic, he liked what he saw and heard.

August A. Busch, III

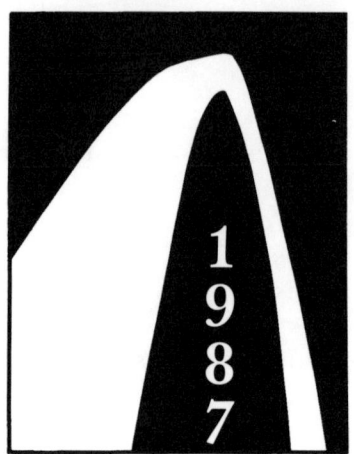

DOWN BY THE RIVERSIDE, south of the throbbing central business district, a city-within-a-city rises out of the fertile St. Louis earth, as flourishing and as meticulously tended as the crops of barley and hops and rice that go into its beer. The seventy-square-block complex of brick and glass and steel has been the working world of August Adolphus Busch III, corporate executive and community leader, chairman of the board and president of Anheuser-Busch Companies, Inc., and chairman of the board and chief executive officer of Anheuser-Busch, Inc., the largest brewing organization in the world.

Thirty miles to the west, near the Mississippi River, corn and soybeans sprout from the rich farm soil and wildfowl flourish in the woodland, the private world of August Busch, outdoorsman, family man, a "farm boy at heart." His downtown office, overlooking the stadium that bears the family name, is only a few hundred yards from the renovated schoolhouse where his father, August A. Busch, Jr., worked at the rolltop desk he inherited from his father, August A. Busch, Sr.

"I want to stress two things," he said, clipping his words and occasionally underlining the point by tapping his finger smartly on the polished table in his office suite.

"Number one, the key is not that August Busch has done something in the community and this company. A group of people has done it. A team of managers makes things happen, not an individual.

"Number two, the person who put us in a position to be able to do the things that we have done, was my father. He is the one who set the base for this corporation and set its standards. We simply picked up the fundamentals and stretched them to more distant horizons."

Still, August A. Busch III is credited with leading the firm through

a dramatic decade of expansion, diversification, and increase in market share since his election to the top leadership post in 1975. Sales of Anheuser-Busch beer brands almost doubled, and the company's market share increased from 22.4 percent to 34.6 percent. Four major labels were introduced during this period, and Budweiser, the company's flagship brand, chalked up unprecedented growth.

His civic involvement paralleled his climb up the corporate ladder, and he gave his name, his time, and his private and corporate resources to health, cultural, and educational institutions and community agencies. He was chairman of the trust fund committee of the Boy Scout Council of Greater St. Louis, chairman of the board of St. John's Mercy Medical Center, a member of the boards of the United Way and Civic Progress. As an industry and community leader, he was on the board of Overseers for the Wharton School, University of Pennsylvania; director emeritus of the School of Business Administration at the college of William and Mary; a director of the General American Life Insurance Company, Southwestern Bell, Emerson Electric, the Beer Institute and Grocery Manufacturers of America.

He received the City of Hope "Spirit of Life" Award, the United States Olympic Committee's "Sports Man of the Year" award and the Mexican-American Legal Defense and Education Fund award for corporate social responsibility. His firm was rated among the "Five Best Managed Companies" by Dun's *Business Month*, and in a 1983 survey by *Fortune Magazine*, Anheuser-Busch was named among the ten most-admired companies in the nation. He was chosen as the 1984 Executive of the Year by Sales and Marketing Executives of St. Louis.

"My father," Busch said with pride, "was the gentleman who first took the brewery system outside of St. Louis. He was the one who took the brewery system to Newark, New Jersey. That was our first expansion, something unheard of in 1951, to make the beers outside of the mother city and the mother plant."

But August A. Busch III has put his unique stamp on the company, just as he has charted his own lifestyle. He was born a son of prestige and privilege, scion of a family dynasty founded well over a century ago by a German immigrant, a sturdy, multi-generational family tree with numerous branches, a spirited and close-knit St. Louis clan that has lived with gusto and given generously to its mother city. Busch traced his St. Louis roots to the marriage of Adolphus Busch, who came from Germany in 1857, and Lilly Anheuser, daughter of Eberhard Anheuser, a wealthy soap manufacturer. Anheuser had taken over the debt-ridden Bavarian Brewery at Broadway and Pestalozzi, and his new son-in-law, on his return from service with the Union Army during the Civil War, was placed in charge.

Anheuser had made an excellent choice. Adolphus Busch was a hearty, gregarious super-salesman with exceptional business acumen. Under his direction, the Anheuser-Busch Brewing Association flourished. Budweiser was introduced as a quality light lager beer and took top honors at international expositions. Adolphus Busch, an imposing, almost legendary figure, was dubbed by St. Louisans, "The First Citizen."

At his death in Germany in 1913, his son, August A. Busch, Sr., became president. But this was the eve of World War I, and soon the beer industry was devastated by Prohibition and, with all businesses, by the dark days of the depression. While many other brewery owners gave up, August, aided by his two young sons, Adolphus III and August, Jr. ("Gussie"), struggled for survival.

"It was a long pull," a *St. Louis Globe-Democrat* reporter wrote, "but father, sons and brewery held together until the dawn of repeal came up at 12:01 o'clock on the morning of April 7, 1933."

A year later, on the death of August A. Busch, Sr., Adolphus took over the presidency. In 1946, after a brief illness, he also died, to be succeeded by Gussie. And so it was that, at the age of nine, young August III, great-grandson of Adolphus and Lilly Anheuser Busch, grandson of August A. Busch, Sr., and son of August A. Busch, Jr., fell into line as heir apparent. He spent his childhood and youth in a spacious home on Lindell Boulevard across from Forest Park, at Grant's farm, and at the farm adjacent to his present 1,000-acre property near St. Charles. He attended Ashland School at Newstead Avenue and Natural Bridge Road and graduated from Ladue High School.

For two years he studied marketing and business at the University of Arizona before spending a year at Seibel Institute of Brewing in Chicago, where he learned the intricacies of brewing, supplementing the knowledge gained from his father and his own summer experience in an assignment in the company's malt house.

"I was about seventeen or eighteen," he recalled. "My first job was throwing out the malt from the germination drums with a pitchfork."

In the mid-1950s, August was in uniform, stationed at Fort Leonard Wood, and subsequently entered a two-year union apprentice program that took him through almost every job in the brewery. In 1962 he joined the company's marketing department, working in the field with wholesalers and at company-based branches throughout the United States. He returned to the St. Louis headquarters as assistant sales manager of regional brands, advanced to sales manager, and in 1963 was named a member of the Anheuser-Busch, Inc., board of directors and appointed vice-president of marketing operations.

Continuing his climb, he became general manager in 1965; executive vice-president and general manager in 1971; president in 1974; chief executive officer in 1975; chairman of the board in 1977; chairman and president of Anheuser-Busch Companies, Inc., in February 1979; chairman of the board and chief executive officer of Anheuser-Busch, Inc., in October 1979. In 1986 he resumed the office of president and chief operating officer of Anheuser-Busch, Inc., in addition to his other duties.

He taught his wife, Ginny, to fly. "In this family, everybody flies," she said. Busch's daily sky journey has been the invisible thread that tied together the two halves of his life.

The moment the big bird nestled on the helipad on the company roof, August Busch, in conservative business attire, white shirt, and, frequently, boots was at work in an all-consuming corporate world. The moment it rested a few feet from the front door of his spacious, custom-designed home in the isolation of the country, he changed to khakis and sport shirt and became again the family man, the outdoorsman, the farmer.

"My father instilled in all of us that quality is the cornerstone of success," said Busch. "If you have been at Busch Gardens, you have the seen the quality of the service and the presentation. If you have been at the stadium, you will say that it is a quality operation, from the cleanliness of the place and the way in which it has been redone and refurbished, to the quality of the people who serve you there.

"He also taught me that the business relationships with our wholesalers are extremely important."

But what about August III? What have been his contributions? The answer was swift and decisive, without self-aggrandizement. "We have not changed the product from my father's day. We have modernized facilities to increase productivity. It costs us more to make a bottle of Budweiser than it costs any other brewer in the country because of our process and because of our ingredients.

"About seventy percent of the people in our company are shareholders, so they have an interest in how the corporation is functioning, what the profitability is, what the competition is doing," said Busch. Once he sent to middle and upper managers and wholesalers a personalized name plate for each one's desk. On the reverse side was the message: "Other than the quality of our products, the most important thing we have is each other."

What does he think of the economy? What of America's future? What of his native St. Louis?

"The future of America is bright," he said. "We need to focus on a few things. But this country's ingenuity, entrepreneurial attitude and structure in the free enterprise system, needless to say, are the best in the world and will continue to be that. We need open and free communications and the ability to trade in other countries. I'm not sure that at all times we do have as open and free ability to trade in other countries as those countries have to trade here. This seems to be something we should be looking at in the future."

What are St. Louis' strengths and weaknesses?

"Most of them are strengths. I don't see many weaknesses. It is a cohesive community, by and large. It works well together. That is evidenced by looking at what is happening downtown and the great expansion in St. Louis County and the metro area.

"There is good leadership in this town. There are many fine corporate leaders, many good people who like this city. Look at what was done years ago when leaders such as my father and Dave Calhoun and Wes McAfee and Dude Chambers, Ted Jones, Buck Persons, Edgar Queeny, George Capps, and the Danforth family turned the course for the city. That was when the downtown development came in. That was when the corner was turned to put St. Louis in the direction we see it following today."

Robert Hyland

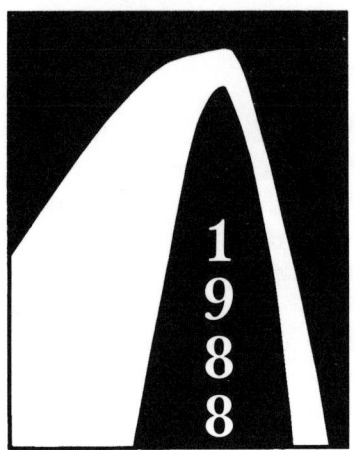

ROBERT HYLAND CREATED ONE CAREER out of thin air. The other grew out of his lifelong love affair with his hometown. Hyland was a broadcaster, a dominant national leader in the broadcast industry whose innovative ideas were recognized and copied by stations across the country. He has also been a Renaissance civic activist whose ideas, energy and enterprise were reflected in institutions, agencies, and programs across the St. Louis area.

As a young man, Hyland could have gone into that exciting new medium called television. He could have become an actor, an athlete or the Number One man of major network. But those choices would have taken him from the microphone to the camera, to Hollywood, to New York, or on the road.

He chose instead to stay right where he was. Having made that decision, he went to work in St. Louis, becoming senior vice-president of CBS Radio and general manager of KMOX and KLOU-FM Radio, the CBS-owned stations in St. Louis. To that prestigious post, he devoted the major portion of his eighteen-hour day—a day that began at 1 A.M. and continued into the early evening. The rest of his time he gave to St. Louis. For both segments of his public, professional life, he adhered to the same philosophy: If you have a job to do, do it. Give it your best shot. Then move on to the next one.

The job he took on in broadcasting was to create a new role for radio in the burgeoning media mix. Everyone laughed when he sat down to work. Radio, they pointed out, was in its twilight years. Hyland knew he was taking a risk, but with "true grit" and the entrepreneurial spirit of Henry Ford, he launched a career that linked the golden age and the space age. He transformed KMOX, and much of the radio industry,

from a listening post into a give-and-take public forum with "At Your Service" call-in programs through much of the day and night, augmenting the staff with an army of specialists in a variety of fields.

Listeners from all over the country, as far as the station's 50,000-watt signal could reach, called to ask questions or air their views. High-ranking authorities, distinguished government leaders, experts in a hundred fields, have taken part in the wide-ranging conversations. As one station commercial promises, "If you think about it, we'll probably talk about it."

Even though he lived and worked in a world of sound, Hyland also initiated the confidential, off-the-air "Call for Action," volunteer service programs offering assistance to individuals across the area, steering them to appropriate community resources.

And in another bold move, he built a bridge across the globe via satellite to connect his own listener/participants to their counterparts on Radio Moscow and set up an exchange not among high-level diplomats but among plain human beings.

"We will get to know them better," he said. " We'll talk about issues that are important to them just as they are important to us."

Regarding the evolution in radio and the "new" medium, television, Hyland said, "The great programs on radio were finding their way into television, so radio had to do one of two things—play records to fill the time or be innovative and try to be different. I felt that if I were going to be in the business, I would not sit there and play records. There is nothing wrong with that, but I had a different philosophy. I thought at that time people wanted to be informed. Radio was just a monologue. Why not let them talk to us and find out what they were interested in?

"Many people in the broadcasting business thought I was nuts. They said I would fall on my face, that we would be out of business in thirty days and I probably would be out of a job. I said, no, I thought this was the right thing and the right time. That's how it turned out."

Professional achievement has not been enough for Hyland. "If you live in a community," he said, "I think your responsibility is not only to be employed there. You must participate in activities for your community's welfare."

Few community leaders have been involved in so many programs and projects. Few, if any, have achieved more. He was chairman of the St. Louis Regional Commerce and Growth Association, chairman of Downtown St. Louis and chairman of the board of Lindenwood College, president of the Missouri Broadcasters Association, chairman of the St. Louis Regional Medical Center, president of the St. Louis Zoological Commission, a member of Civic Progress, chairman of the board of St. Anthony's Medical Center, and founder of the Hyland Center for the treatment of alcoholism and drug abuse within the St. Anthony's medical complex. He was chairman of the Municipal Theater Association and headed its fiftieth anniversary committee. He was elected for an unprecedented four-year term and was instrumental in developing a new format, featuring productions directly from Broadway.

He was named to the Missouri Academy of Squires. Missouri Governor John Ashcroft and Illinois Governor James Thompson named him to the Bi-State panel on bridges, and he also served as chairman of the Jefferson National Expansion Memorial Association. He was on the board of the major case squad of greater St. Louis, was chairman of Old Newsboys Day in 1976, vice president of the St. Louis Area Council of the Boy Scouts of America, and chairman of the steering committee for the annual mayor's prayer breakfast. He served as board member of St. Patrick's Center and was on the board of the St. Louis chapter of the NAACP and the St. Louis Urban League.

He was president of the Media Club and led the development of the club's new quarters atop the Laclede Gas Building. He has been president of the Knights of the Cauliflower Ear, founder and past president of the Stadium Club, past president of the Variety Club, the Advertising Club and of the St. Louis Sports Hall of Fame. He was on the board of Centerre Trust Company and Wetterau, Inc. Through long hours and indefatigable energy, he combined these activities with building KMOX into the number one station in the nation's largest metropolitan areas.

A devout Roman Catholic, he received the commendation of Magistral Knight of the Sovereign Military Order of Malta by Pope Paul VI, and an honorary doctor of laws degrees from Lindenwood College and the University of Missouri-St Louis, as well as an honorary doctor of public service degree from his alma mater, Saint Louis University. He received the prestigious St. Louis Award for outstanding contributions to the community; the Right Arm of St. Louis Award from the RCGA; the Henry Shaw Award from the Missouri Botanical Gardens; the Abe Lincoln Award from the Southern Baptist Radio and Television Commission; and the American Advertising Federation silver medal award.

He was named "Outstanding Young Man of St. Louis" by the Junior Chamber of Commerce, "Business Leader of the Year" by the Harvard Business School Club, Sales Executive of the Year by the Sales and Marketing Executives of Greater St. Louis, and Media Person of the Year by the Press Club of Metropolitan St. Louis. He received the Silver Beaver Award for distinguished service to youth by the Boy Scouts of America.

"Bob Hyland has had a very distinguished business career, operating one of, if not the most, successful radio stations in the country,'" said former Laclede Gas Company chairman Lee M. Liberman.

"What a unique man he is!" said Ted C. Wetterau. "He is behind many major projects and has spent more time helping than anyone I know."

Three times Hyland turned down invitations to become president of CBS Radio in favor of being "the voice of St. Louis."

"That was my ambition," he said, "to be president of the network. But the first time I was asked, my first wife was dying. The second and third times, I was too involved with St. Louis, and I didn't want to leave."

He was speaking of the late Martha Claiborne Hyland, the mother of his two eldest sons, Robert F., III, called Rip, and the late William Claiborne, known as Clay, both in their early teens when they lost their mother. Several years after her death, Hyland married the former Patricia Sowle, and their two children are Molly and Matthew. He didn't talk much about his private thoughts and dreams, and he didn't parade the strong religious faith that motivated him to cross to the Old Cathedral for Mass every morning. The portrait of Robert Hyland must be painted by his associates, his employees, and his friends.

"He has had a sixth sense about programming and personnel. He has seldom mismatched 'At Your Service' teams, but he knew right away if he made a mistake and was quick to remedy it. He's unique," said sports announcer Jack Buck, one of his closest friends. "There has never been anybody like him, never will be. His imagination, his foresightedness, his tenacity, his purpose of mind. I have seen him when he put his teeth into a project like St. Anthony's or the Zoo or the Muny. I know he doesn't do it for self-aggrandizement. He has done a pretty good job of staying out of the limelight. I am 100 percent certain he doesn't want it."

Buck's words were underlined by Bob Costas. "If I were to make a list of people who have done the most for me professionally, he would be at the top," said the sportscaster/host who, like Buck, is heard on the network as well as on local broadcasts. "He gave me a tremendous amount of guidance both as a professional and as a person. It has been almost a father-son relationship. I would not have gone to New York had he not urged me to pursue whatever was best for me."

Hyland attended Barat Hall, a private Catholic boys' school, graduated from Saint Louis University High School and Saint Louis University.

His was a privileged life, a social life of debutante parties and travel. But, from his father, the late Dr. Robert F. Hyland, prominent surgeon who pioneered in sports medicine, he inherited a serious commitment to his work and a habit of continuing to study and learn.

"I remember my father as one of the most successful surgeons in the country. He always studied to keep up with his profession. I do that too. The morning is my quiet time for that. Nobody bothers me here. I require little sleep, only four or five hours."

His mother, he said, was a "marvelous, beautiful, outgoing person," who, with Dr. Hyland, exerted a strong influence on their son. His radio career began in sales and on the air in smaller stations for CBS in Chicago before he returned to St. Louis to begin his climb up the managerial ladder at KMOX.

In 1973, after fourteen years as vice president of CBS and general manager of KMOX and KMOX-FM (now KLOU), he was named regional vice-president of CBS—the first such designation in the CBS organization.

"I attribute his growth in his profession," said a colleague, "to a tremendous sense of what the audience wants and needs. He has a real sensitivity to that."

Hyland, who had grown up with Jack Armstrong, the all-American boy, Little Orphan Annie, and the Green Hornet, reluctantly admitted that his imaginary heroes' days were numbered and began to find other ways for radio to serve the public. A long list of "firsts" was the result.

"Communication in space will come," he said. "There will be interplanetary travel to this great unknown, and we have to explore. That's what this was when we started our 'At Your Service' format nearly thirty years ago. It was a new frontier in broadcasting. If you are going to be a citizen in today's world, it is vital that you keep informed."

What does he see in that society, and what does he envision, not only for his home town but for his country?

"St. Louis is one of the best kept secrets in the world. It is not only a big city. It is also a small town. You can move around and get to know people from all walks of life. This is what gives it a community flavor. We know each other and our problems. We have our squabbles, but even though they are intense, they are usually good-natured. We are all trying to do the same thing, to make this a better community, to attract more industry.

"I would like to see an arrangement where the county could become more of the city and vice-versa. If we could become one community, we could progress a lot farther. I realize the county's problems because

I live there. But if somehow we could all work together even more closely, it would be better. I have some reservations about light rail. We have so many luxuries in our automobiles that I wonder if people will use it. But I have seen its success in other cities. We have to give a lot more time and attention to education. There will be more demands in industry for people coming to work. Education is the way to go."

Hyland didn't believe that the country was about ready to self-destruct, but he was disheartened about its lowered morality.

"It's terrible. It's an indictment of us as a people. I know we all can't walk as saints, but neither can we walk around as we are today. I am not a preacher or a Johnny-do-good, but this must get someone's attention. The drug situation is beyond belief. But freedom and opportunity still exist in this country. As crowded as we are, and as many wrong things going on, there are new horizons. We are becoming very global and this is exciting."

What does he expect this world to be like in the year 2000? He wasn't certain, but he hoped to live to see it. And he had no plans to retire. There was too much left for Robert Hyland to tackle.

Robert F. Hyland, Jr., died on March 5, 1992.

Peter H. Raven

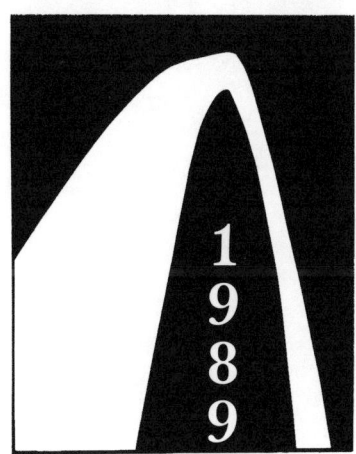

PETER HAMILTON RAVEN'S SPECIAL WORLD has been a woodland retreat in the heart of the city, an island of tranquility he transformed into a garden without walls which kept on growing across the globe.

This is the renowned Missouri Botanical Garden, and Raven, its director and catalyst. Every morning, just as the dawn seeped into the dark, he stepped briskly up the flagstone path from his home to his office in the Lehmann Building to continue his battle against the forces of evil that would degrade, desecrate, and destroy the land, especially the rain forests of the tropics, the world's lush vegetation essential to human survival.

Raven's greatest worry has been about human population growth, "which has taken us from 2.5 billion in 1950 to 5.2 billion and is headed for fourteen billion by the end of the next century. Of the 2.7 billion people in developing countries outside of China," he continued, "the World Bank estimates that one billion live in extreme poverty—that's one out of five in the world—and that 500 million receive less than eighty percent of the United Nations' recommended minimum dietary allowance, which means that their minds and bodies can't develop properly. Some thirteen million of them are babies under the age of four who starve to death or die of disease related to starvation every year—about 36,000 a day."

When Peter Raven was a boy, he collected butterflies and beetles. He grew into a man of international renown, a scholar, writer, innovator, environmentalist, ecologist, social activist, adviser to prelate and emperor, an ebullient leader who transformed "Mr. Shaw's Garden" into a world-class institution and research center.

With the deft hands of a surgeon, he gave the venerable dowager a

major facelift, smoothed out the wrinkles left by time and inadequate funds, and reintroduced her to St. Louis, indeed to the world.

Before assuming his heavy administrative duties, Raven, described by an interviewer as "a man of catalytic energy," sometimes journeyed to the tropics to collect plants and to add to his own vast reservoir of scientific information. With his inborn sense of adventure and hunger for knowledge, he was as much at home in the mud and heat of the rain forest as in the executive suite, in prestigious halls where he was honored, or in the presence of dignitaries who visited the Garden.

Raven, a descendant of men and women who joined the Donner Party in 1846 to fight their way across the western frontier to California, had his own frontiers to conquer. "In botany, there are many frontiers," he explained, "such as the plants that provide the food we eat directly or indirectly. And those are diminishing. We are going backward. That is the kind of problem that the garden tries to address."

Raven received numerous honorary doctorates from eight American and foreign universities. He was elected to illustrious academies of science in America, Denmark, Sweden, New Zealand, Italy, Russia, and India. His prestigious awards include: International Prize for Biology, government of Japan; International Environmental Leadership medal, United Nations; Wildenow medal, Berlin Botanical Garden; foreign member, Linnean Society of London; Distinguished Service Award, American Institute of Biological Sciences; honorary president of the Third National Congress of Botany.

In addition to his directorship of the Missouri Botanical Garden, he became the Englemann Professor of Botany at Washington University—a tenure appointment for the Garden's administrator—and adjunct professor of biology both at Saint Louis University and the University of Missouri at St. Louis.

He was named home secretary of the National Academy of Sciences; chairman of the report review committee, National Research Council; member of the committee on research and exploration, National Geographic Society; president of the International Organization of Plant Biosystematics; member of the Smithsonian Council; on the education advisory board of the John Simon Guggenheim Memorial Foundation; and chairman of the Conservation International Chairmen's Council.

Raven is not without honor in his own community. He served on the board of curators of the University of Missouri; was a commissioner of Tower Grove Park; and was the recipient of the John D. Levy Human Relations Award from St. Louis chapter, the American Jewish Committee. In 1988 he received the St. Louis Award.

Raven was never one to sit down complacently and watch the world swirl around him or stay in the ivory tower of classroom or laboratory, protected from the frontline battle. From childhood he was an adventurer, endowed with a sense of wonder. In his adult years, like a twentieth-century Don Quixote, he sharpened that inquiring mind with a sense of outrage at what was happening to his world.

His boyhood was spent in California, which has been the family home for four generations. Early in the century, his great-uncle established a bank, a real estate firm, and other businesses in Shanghai. He then persuaded his brother to come to China to manage two of the companies.

The brother's teen-aged son, Walter Francis Raven, who became Peter's father, finished high school there, then returned to the United States to enter the University of Santa Clara. He met his future wife, Isabelle Breen, at the University of California in Berkeley.

The couple settled in Shanghai, where Peter was born on June 13, 1936. But the depression had reached the Orient, and the young family returned to San Francisco, where Peter was destined to take his first steps on the scientific road. When he was two years old, his father introduced him to the California Academy of Sciences Museum, an institution that, in time, would become the boy's second home. When he was seven, he was transporting caterpillars in his little red wagon and bringing into his bed grasshoppers tied together with thread—a practice his mother quickly discouraged.

"By the time I was six or eight," Raven said, "I was interested in natural history, in birds and snakes and plants, all of that. I think most kids are somewhat interested at that age.

"The question is not so much how a child becomes interested, but why most of them stop exploring," said Raven. "In my case, I stayed. When I was eight, I joined the student section of the California Academy of Sciences in San Francisco. That was a very encouraging kind of environment, where you could immediately feel that what you were doing was worthwhile.

"By the time I was in high school," he said, "I knew this would be my career, and when I was a college freshman I thought perhaps I would be a teacher. Then I learned about other possibilities."

Raven spent his first two years at the University of San Francisco, then transferred to the University of California at Berkeley, where he graduated with highest honors. After taking his doctorate from the University of California in Los Angeles, he was selected as a National Science Foundation Postdoctoral Fellow at the British Museum, studying plants he had worked on in his graduate studies in deserts of the western United States and northwestern Mexico.

In turn, he became taxonomist and curator of the herbarium of Rancho Santa Ana Botanic Garden; assistant, then associate professor of biological sciences at Stanford University. On a sabbatical from Stanford, he and his wife, Tamra, spent 1969 and 1970 in New Zealand studying plant life.

"In the late 1960s," he said, "I was becoming interested in human population growth and the human impact on the environment. I was interested loosely in conservation before that, but I had no idea of the human pressures on the environment."

Gradually, his research turned to the tropics. In 1959, as a graduate student at UCLA, he had gone to Colombia on a study trip and in the early 1960s had begun working on the folk taxonomy of the Tzeltal Indians of Chipas in southern Mexico, to learn how they were dealing with plants.

In 1967 that interest was heightened when he went to Costa Rica with the Organization on Tropical Studies, a consortium of forty universities, as instructor in botany and ecology. In 1971, when Raven at thirty-five was already a distinguished scientist, he was appointed to head the Missouri Botanical Garden. He was prepared to enhance its reputation for research as well as for exhibition, and he hit the grounds running—his normal way of confronting a new challenge, whatever the job.

Within a few months of his appointment, he was asked by the National Science Foundation to chair a committee to advise about the future of systematic and evolutionary biology. He convened about thirty-five people here.

"We came up with two answers which have been very much themes of the way I have felt since," said Raven. "One, the building of data bases is extremely important because the amount of available information is so large that unless that could be done sensibly, we wouldn't be getting anywhere.

"Two, plants, animals, and microorganisms were being destroyed so rapidly in the tropics that we needed to concentrate a lot of our attention there if we were going to have any chance of describing or dealing with them or using them for human benefit while they were still around."

Though he spoke with authority and conviction on world issues, the real heart of Peter Raven's life was the home he has shared with his family—a large, sturdy brick dwelling on the Garden property that has been occupied by each director since 1914. Books are everywhere. Plants, many of them rare orchids—Raven's favorites—add their beauty to each room.

During a visit to St. Louis, his mother, Isabelle Raven, spoke of Peter's childhood. "He was never a mischievous child, never in trouble. We didn't try to push him toward a career. We encouraged him in whatever he wanted to do. He didn't have pets, as we lived right in the city, and anyway, he liked beetles and other bugs better."

Tamra Raven, with a master's degree in ecology and a gifted scientist in her own right, is Peter's second wife and the mother of Francis and Katie. Peter and Tamra, who had met earlier on the tropical studies project in Costa Rica, were married in 1968 after the death of his first wife. Two daughters were born to that first marriage, Alice and Elizabeth.

For Peter, "Mr. Shaw's Garden," with its blossoms and plants and research projects and educational programs and world-renowned collections, with its climatron and herbarium, its exquisite Japanese garden, its statuary, giant trees and shaded walks, and aura of peace was always a retreat.

"Most of the buildings and plants known to Henry Shaw have been replaced by more modern structures, newly developed horticultural varieties or newly discovered species of wild plants," Raven wrote in *A World of Plants*, the handsomely illustrated story of the Garden published by Abrams in 1989.

"The Garden is a world of plants, a living museum devoted to their display, to educating people about them and to research to increase our knowledge about them.

"We have the largest program working with tropical plants of any organization in the world. Our ability to use those plants will be decisive for the future of hundreds of millions of people.

"We have only a quarter of a million kinds of plants in the world, which is a lot on one hand but, on the other, not very many when you realize how total and complete is our dependence on them. Only about 300 are in worldwide commerce, and only about 5,000 have been used widely as crops.

"The world of the future will be one inevitably in which nations will cooperate more closely with one another. . . . There will be more of a conscious realization of a community interest in what happens to the whole world and when that time comes, we will be a lot better off. . . .

"Internationalism, ecologically sound living, and exercising democracy—those are the most important things."

Donald O. Schnuck

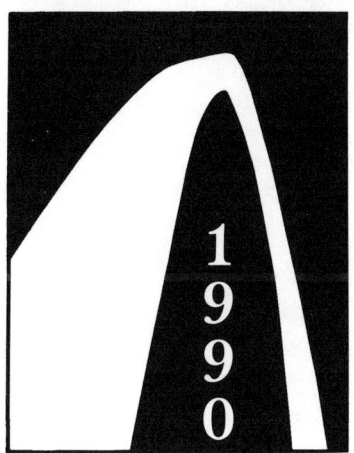

IT WAS ONE OF THOSE CORNER GROCERY STORES that were so much a part of St. Louis a half-century ago. Friendly little gathering places—not fancy or flamboyant—some of them as old-fashioned as a pot-bellied stove and penny candy and oatmeal; they were the sinew of the city, helping knit neighborhoods together. Schnuck's confectionery at Warne and Labadie was just such a place, opened in 1939 by Anna Donovan "Mom" Schnuck, a family enterprise fueled by faith and maintained by hard work and ingenuity on the part of Edwin H. and Anna Schnuck and their three children, Edward J., Annette, and Donald.

Out of that congenial little mecca, in more than fifty years of acquiring existing stores and opening new ones, of risk-taking and "making do," of successes and disappointments, of old-fashioned customer service and innovative merchandising, evolved Schnuck Markets, Inc. And out of this warm-hearted corner of the world in north St. Louis came Donald O. Schnuck, youngest of that sturdy clan and eventual corporate chairman of Schnuck Markets. The teenage helper in the store a half-century ago became a leader in his community and his industry, who, with his cherished wife, watched with unabashed pride the achievements of their sons and daughter.

Even after he had grown gray and affluent with the years, Don Schnuck never went far, in his mind, from the little north St. Louis confectionery and the early family stores that succeeded it. His older brother, Ed, who died in 1987, and his sister, Mrs. Raymond Handhardt, followed the principles of merchandising and personal customer service that evolved as their enterprise developed.

Donald was a gentle activist, a self-effacing pacesetter and entrepreneur who respected gut feelings but carried computer data in his hip pocket,

an honored mover and shaker who ate in the company cafeteria and was called Don by most of the firm's employees. As the firm expanded, so did his own horizons. Through the years, he shared his business acumen with his parents, his brother and sister, and, in turn, with his sons.

But Schnuck also shared his time and energy with his city and its people, subscribing to the company's mission statement that reads in part: "We will fulfill our civic responsibilities to our community by corporate and individual involvement in those organizations and activities that make a positive attempt to benefit the development, growth and quality of life in our marketing areas. We will attempt to provide the appropriate support to those agencies and organizations that attend to the needs of those sectors of our society that require assistance."

Craig, Don's eldest son, led the effort to create the mission statement. He recognized the importance of documenting the principles and traditions that made the Schnuck organization what it is.

A man of his word, Don Schnuck was both a generalist and specialist in his civic philanthropy, both a representative of his company and a private citizen. Accepting the traditional mantle of top St. Louis executives as a catalyst in community wide activities, he served as chairman of the 1986 United Way campaign and chairman of the 1988 Salvation Army Tree of Lights. He was on the executive committee of the United Way and a member of Civic Progress. In 1988 he led the successful community-wide campaign to make the History Museum a part of the zoo-museum tax district.

He was particularly proud of the key role he played in the $54 million St. Louis County bond issue in 1969. It made possible the present county park system, including acquisition of Queeny Park, the Children's Juvenile Center in Clayton, the three county recreations centers and the vast road improvements that are the foundation of today's county road system.

Schnuck also maintained a thick portfolio of personal commitments. Among these were St. Louis Children's Hospital, Junior Achievement, John Burroughs School (his children's alma mater), the YMCA, the History Museum, the Boy Scouts, and the Girl Scouts. He was board chairman or president of the hospital, Junior Achievement and John Burroughs, was on the advisory committee of the YMCA and the board of the Missouri Historical Society. He served on innumerable other civic groups.

Don received the Herman F. Spoehrer Award for his dedication and service to Junior Achievement and an honorary doctor of laws degree from Maryville College. "Initially," according to the company's fiftieth anniversary history, "Ed dedicated much of his time to the firm's community efforts. The organization's benevolence in sharing its management talent was expanded later to include Don's services in community leadership, as Schnucks developed a cadre of talented managers that allowed significant donations of both Ed's and Don's time and talent to the community.

After Edward's death, Don assumed sole responsibility for corporate giving and, although he preferred to keep a low profile, his role as a community catalyst continued to grow. "I never did get into any activity because I was looking for something at the end of the rainbow," he said. "It was always something I believed in."

He began college but wasn't destined to graduate from Washington University. Uncle Sam saw to that. Before completing his undergraduate work, he joined the Navy College Training Program, was sent to Washburn University in Topeka, Kansas, then to midshipman's school at Columbia University, and was commissioned as an ensign on December 15, 1944. He also studied in the communications school at Harvard and probably could have gone on to language school and a place in an American embassy, but St. Louis was his home, and this was where he wanted to be.

Four days after receiving his commission, Ensign Schnuck returned to St. Louis and the family church—now Friedens United Church of Christ—to marry Doris Letson, his bubbly schoolmate at Beaumont High School, the daughter of Charles Letson, a captain in the St. Louis Fire Department. His father, anticipating Don's return from service and hoping he would want to stay in the retail food business, had bought for the couple an old-time service grocery at 5389 Geraldine Avenue near Walnut Park. That store on Geraldine was the beginning of Don Schnuck's career as an owner-manager. Gradually over the years, he, his father, and brother began to build the family food business.

All the family members began as baggers or in other entry level jobs and worked their way up the ladder, learning at their dad's insistence, every facet of the business. Sharing the sons' place in his heart—if not in the business—was his daughter, Nancy, a media planner at D'Arcy Masius Benton & Bowles.

Doris met her future husband at a De Molay dance, gave up her job as a checker at their first store to care for her growing family and agreed with Don that her place was at home as a full-time mother. "If I have had any blessing," Don once said, "it is that Doris is my wife and the mother of my children."

Thanksgiving and Christmas—Don's favorite times—always found them in St.Louis, close to their clan. More than thirty-five of them gathered around the table for Thanksgiving dinner and around the Christmas tree for gift-giving.

Living and working in the world of food, Schnuck could enjoy its finest delicacies, but among his favorites were sauerkraut and spareribs, beef stew, home-made soups, prime steaks, and hot fudge sundaes. Unless he had a board or committee meeting outside the office, he always had lunch with his employees in the company cafeteria.

Schnuck felt a special interest in Children's Hospital because some of his children were patients many years before, and several grandchildren have used its services. Once Don was named to the board, he became a dedicated worker. He was on the board when the new $50 million structure was built and, in November 1983, as chairman, he laid the cornerstone.

Loving children and young people, and loving his country and its system of government with a patriotic zeal, Schnuck quite naturally became involved with Junior Achievment. "Organizations such as Junior Achievement, the Scouts, and YMCA teach young people the right values, raise them to be healthy-minded citizens," he said.

Schnuck was a staunch conservative and active in the Republican party. He was on a first-name basis with Governor John Ashcroft, Senator Christopher Bond, and many other state and national leaders. While he could not list any heroes, he singled out Dwight Eisenhower as a leader for whom he had deep respect. Among his treasures was an autographed picture of himself and Doris with then vice-president, George Bush. Another is autographed "to Doris and Don, best wishes, Ronald Reagan," a rememberance from a state dinner at the White House.

Even though he climbed the ladder on his own and had a strong belief in individual responsibility, Schnuck would not deny help for those who could not make it.

"We have to take care of the sick and infirm in our society," he said. "I am not conservative to the point where I don't think we should have Medicare or hospitalization for everyone. Somehow, we have to find a way to do that without dragging down the whole country in the process. Health care costs are rising faster than our ability to pay, but we do need to provide health care for our whole society. It is morally right."

If he had been in the White House or in the Congress, what would he have done to solve America's problems?

"Deficit spending will have to be reduced if our country is to remain viable from an economic standpoint, particularly in a global sense. We aren't just an island sitting out on the North American continent with everything that the rest of the world doesn't have. The rest of the world is catching up with us, and we are going to need to get our own house in order and match productivity with the rest of the world if we are to maintain the proper standard of living for the people of this country."

But given today's conditions, is there still opportunity? Could the Schnuck family start over with a small grocery and build a food empire? Again came the strong answer.

"Yes. It may even be easier today than it was over fifty years ago. Desire and hard work are the main ingredients. Naturally, a basic amount of intelligence is important. My family had an entrepreneurial perspective and, at the same time, was mindful of the respect due others and the dignity of the individual."

Donald O. Schnuck died on June 17, 1991.

William E. Cornelius

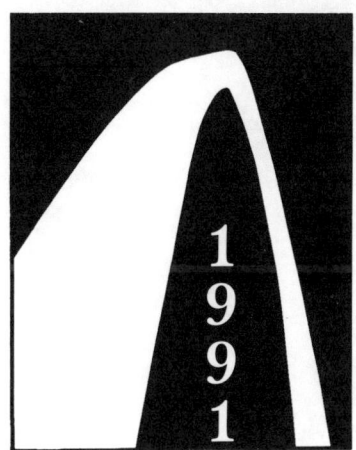

B ILL CORNELIUS, A MAN OF BUSINESS AND FAITH, was a Mizzou football player who returned to school thirty years later for a graduate degree, an ex-army lieutenant who wrote his thesis about nuclear submarines and taught courses in nuclear weapons and foreign policy. A sociable but unassuming executive, he often introduced himself as "working for Union Electric." A nationally known leader in the electric utility industry, he helped keep the lights turned on in three states; a civic activist, he made sure St. Louis' special aura as a great city didn't dim.

William Edward Cornelius has been president of Civic Progress, board chairman of St. Louis Children's Hospital, trustee of Washington University, chairman of the Muny, and a director of Boatmen's Bancshares, General American Life Insurance Co., Interco Inc. and McDonnell Douglas Corporation. He served on the boards of the Mercantile Library, the Missouri Chamber of Commerce, St. Louis Regional Commerce and Growth Association, and William Woods College. He was a member of the Partnership for Progress CEO Council at the University of Missouri-St. Louis.

He has headed with notable success major fund-raising efforts for St. Louis Children's Hospital, United Way, Arts and Education Council, and the Alliance for Washington University.

A transplant from the west side of the state, Cornelius long ago became an unabashed St. Louis loyalist who, in a colleague's words, "has done a jillion things for St. Louis." The heart of his day-to-day career has been Union Electric's headquarters.

No word has been more important in Bill Cornelius' vocabulary than "family." He and his wife Ginger are the parents of Jeanie Davis and Lindy Cornelius and the grandparents of Jeanie's three children:

Virginia, Andrew, and Bill's namesake.

The men and women who have worked for Union Electric have been Cornelius' second family, and he frequently took time to note the progress and the problems of each.

No one in his world has had a greater hold on his mind and heart than the St. Louis family without a home—the destitute mother and her children who find a haven in the shelter operated by the Cathedral Mission Society at Bishop Tuttle Memorial in downtown St. Louis. The modest Cornelius would never put it in such lofty terms, but he has been known by the clergy and fellow parishioners at the cathedral as a Christian activist, whose concept of religion is a blend of prayer and pragmatism.

"Lindy, his daughter, is an Episcopal priest," said Dean Michael Allen of Christ Church Cathedral. "I think Bill wanted to walk with her, and I think one reason he came here on that spiritual walk is that our church has women clergy.

"He is a man of great compassion for the homeless, the poor, and the rejected. And he lives out his spiritual life in action. He is at the church every Sunday and he comes regularly to the shelter. Last Thanksgiving, he was in the kitchen cooking grits. He never pushes himself into the limelight."

It was because of that modesty that he wanted to stay anonymous when he returned to college to take courses for his master of liberal arts degree. "None of his classmates knew who he was," said Ginger Cornelius, "until a man saw him on television and yelled, 'Hey, that's Bill. He's in my class!'"

The quality of leadership has been important to Bill Cornelius. He formed his own philosophy of the demands of leadership. That personal creed—a blend of quiet civic loyalty, a deep concern for people, and a pragmatic approach to human hurts and needs—was reflected in his 1988 Coro Foundation Public Affairs address honoring Thomas F. Latzer, retired executive of Pet, Incorporated, and long-time associate of Coro.

"There are no easy solutions to the problems created by a more pluralistic society, a changing economy, and neglect of many aspects of our infrastructure," he said. "However, if we can bring the proper leadership to bear on the problems, I'm confident solutions can be found."

He listed qualities "that successful leaders seem to have in common." Those qualities, say his colleagues, are abundant in the Cornelius character, a reflection of his own leadership in company, church, and community.

"The first is vision. To lead, you must have a clear idea of where you are going and what objective or goal you want to attain. A second quality of leadership is the willingness to take risks. To improve something involves change, and with change there is always the possibilty of a failure. Sucessful leaders cannot be afraid to fail.

"Another quality of leadership is common sense. You don't have to be a genius to be a good leader. But you do need common sense—some grasp of what will work and what will not. Another mark of a leader is energy. Leadership is hard work. It takes a lot of effort to motivate people, to secure resources, to develop plans and perform all the tasks necessary to accomplish a goal.

"Finally, leaders seem to possess a sense of values. Without integrity or ethical standards, the other qualities I've mentioned do not lead to anything worthwhile. We have been blessed in having many leaders who have put the common good ahead of all else; leaders who have raised the level of the debate to a higher plane. One of the positive things about St. Louis is the degree to which our business leaders have joined with others to find solutions to the social problems facing the less fortunate in this community. We must continue and expand that important tradition."

Born September 6, 1931, in Salt Lake City, where his father, a salesman, was assigned, Cornelius moved with his family to several cities in the Midwest and South. His high school years were spent in Lee's Summit, near Kansas City, not many miles from the region where his ancestors settled after the War of 1812. It was a happy and close family circle—Bill, his parents, and his sister, Linda Dempsey, who became the wife of a physician in Lee's Summit.

Bill played football at Lee's Summit High School, then went to the University of Missouri on a football scholarship, where he played two years as a defensive end in "those dark days of Tiger football." He studied political science and business adminstration and pledged Beta Theta Pi.

"I started out to be an engineer," he recalled, "but when I took chemistry and other science courses, I decided that was not for me. I switched to business and took enough accounting courses to get a job."

In 1953, with a bachelor of science degree in business and public administration, he and his bride, the former Mary Virginia (Ginger) Bunker, went to Germany for a two-year stay. Their older daughter, Jeanie, was born there. Ginger, described by one admirer of the Cornelius family as "Bill's greatest asset," is the daughter of the late Herbert

Bunker, one of the two athletes in the history of Mizzou to earn four letters in sports.

"Bill became interested in the American Indians," said Ginger with a smile, "and read everything he could on that subject. Then it was the Civil War period. He goes from period to period to period."

"St. Louis is a friendly place," Cornelius said. "Ginger and I are beneficiaries of that. We have been made to feel very much at home. A lot of people took an interest in us. David Calhoun was on the Union Electric board when I was a young officer. He always went out of his way to keep in touch."

"Bill said he always felt lucky to work for people who gave credit to the young people who worked for them," said Ginger. "I think that is the kind of boss he is. It made a difference in his career to have that happen and to be given opportunities, and when he did something to have the person above him say, 'I didn't do it—he did it.'"

For his company and its employees, Cornelius instituted such practices as strategic and five-year planning, a flex-time program, a quality improvement program, and incentives for all employees based on quantitative performance improvement. He also established a goal to improve job satisfaction for all employees, to motivate people to achieve a high level of quality in their work. It was important to him that Union Electric be a customer-oriented company, providing energy at the lowest possible cost.

Cornelius has been proud of the company's Callaway nuclear power plant completed during the year he became CEO. "Callaway has an excellent safety record, a good operation. It is a cost-effective plant, with an emphasis on quality throughout its construction."

As though he were looking through a glass that kept magnifying the view, widening the scope, Cornelius turned his thoughts from his company to his community and to his country. "We can only prosper as the community we serve prospers," he said.

And how can that community be improved?

"One of the major things we need to work on is regional cooperation. We have a lot of problems because of political boundaries. Most of our social problems are in the city. Most of our resources are in the county. You have to try to match them up.

"The boundaries probably will not disappear, but there has to be more regional cooperation on some of the major issues. We have started that with Regional Medical Center. The Convention Center represents the first time that the city, the county, and the state have worked jointly on a project.

"One area in which I think we could really make an impact and build a model for the whole country is the area of primary health care for children. So many families depend upon clinics, and the present system doesn't really meet their needs. Many clinics are not open at night. Many operate by appointment only. Kids don't get sick by appointment. Emergency rooms are fine, but it is more cost-effective to have preventive medicine."

If he were president, what would he do about the country?

"I don't think you can expect any one president to solve our problems, but right now, we somehow have to get the deficit under control." A normally optimistic man, Cornelius continued, "America is still the strongest country in the world, but we do have our problems. Remember, though, that we take on a lot of things that other countries do not."

Then Cornelius focused his thoughts on his company. "We have tried to make it easier for customers to do business with us. If you call up with a problem, we try to solve it. One of our problems has been our rates. We are right now at about the midpoint among large cities. We haven't increased our rates since 1987.

"The second complaint is about lights going out. We tried to improve our record of restoring power."

Then, for the moment, Bill Cornelius was not a CEO nor an advocate for the homeless, but a customer of Union Electric.

He laughed at the memory. "Our own lights went out at three in the afternoon a few weeks ago. They were off all night. It was a good experience for me. I called at 8 A. M. and asked if everyone had lights restored.

" Oh, yeah," I was told. " We have everything all cleared up."

"Not quite," I said, "you have one left. Me."